Shitstorm-Prävention

Die Leuphana Case Studies sind ein Projekt, das in Zusammenarbeit mit kleinen und mittelständischen Unternehmen erstellt und entwickelt worden ist. Sie sind ein Lehrbuch, mit dessen Hilfe Unternehmen, die vor ähnlichen Herausforderungen stehen, selbige bewältigen können. Dafür ist keine Hilfe von Dritten notwendig. Auf Grundlage der einzelnen Case Studies werden den Bearbeiterinnen und Bearbeitern elementare Werkzeuge aus der wissenschaftlichen Theorie erklärt. Diese können sie anwenden, um mit den Insiderkenntnissen des eigenen Unternehmens Prozesse zu optimieren, Ziele entwickeln und erreichen oder schwierige Herausforderungen zu bewältigen.

Weitere Bände in dieser Reihe
http://www.springer.com/series/15432
Massonne, Veranstaltungsmanagement - 978-3-662-54003-9
Klöppner et al., Fachkräftemangel im Pflegesektor - 978-3-662-54013-8
Melles, Produkteinführung - 978-3-662-54001-5
Deharde, Produktionsentscheidung - 978-3-662-53997-2
Sikkenga, Shitstorm-Prävention - 978-3-662-54015-2
Göse, Sozialunternehmen - 978-3-662-54007-7
van Hueth et al., Sozialwirtschaft - 978-3-662-54005-3
Giese, Großprojektmanagement - 978-3-662-54011-4
Göse/Reihlen, Gründung einer Unternehmensberatung - 978-3-662-54009-1

Jörg Sikkenga

Shitstorm-Prävention

Jörg Sikkenga
Case Studies
Leuphana Universität Lüneburg
Lüneburg
Deutschland

ISBN 978-3-662-54015-2   ISBN 978-3-662-54016-9 (eBook)
DOI 10.1007/978-3-662-54016-9

Die Deutsche Nationalbibliothek verzeichnet diese Publikation in der Deutschen Nationalbibliografie; detaillierte bibliografische Daten sind im Internet über http://dnb.d-nb.de abrufbar.

Springer Gabler
© Springer-Verlag GmbH Deutschland 2017
Das Werk einschließlich aller seiner Teile ist urheberrechtlich geschützt. Jede Verwertung, die nicht ausdrücklich vom Urheberrechtsgesetz zugelassen ist, bedarf der vorherigen Zustimmung des Verlags. Das gilt insbesondere für Vervielfältigungen, Bearbeitungen, Übersetzungen, Mikroverfilmungen und die Einspeicherung und Verarbeitung in elektronischen Systemen.
Die Wiedergabe von Gebrauchsnamen, Handelsnamen, Warenbezeichnungen usw. in diesem Werk berechtigt auch ohne besondere Kennzeichnung nicht zu der Annahme, dass solche Namen im Sinne der Warenzeichen- und Markenschutz-Gesetzgebung als frei zu betrachten wären und daher von jedermann benutzt werden dürften.
Der Verlag, die Autoren und die Herausgeber gehen davon aus, dass die Angaben und Informationen in diesem Werk zum Zeitpunkt der Veröffentlichung vollständig und korrekt sind. Weder der Verlag, noch die Autoren oder die Herausgeber übernehmen, ausdrücklich oder implizit, Gewähr für den Inhalt des Werkes, etwaige Fehler oder Äußerungen. Der Verlag bleibt im Hinblick auf geografische Zuordnungen und Gebietsbezeichnungen in veröffentlichten Karten und Institutionsadressen neutral.

Gedruckt auf säurefreiem und chlorfrei gebleichtem Papier

Springer Gabler ist Teil von Springer Nature
Die eingetragene Gesellschaft ist Springer-Verlag GmbH Deutschland
Die Anschrift der Gesellschaft ist: Heidelberger Platz 3, 14197 Berlin, Germany

Vorwort des Herausgebers

Im Rahmen des Regionalentwicklungsprojekts Innovations-Inkubator Lüneburg wurden der Leuphana Universität im Zeitraum 2009 bis 2015 Mittel der Europäischen Union und des Landes Niedersachsen zur intensiven Förderung der Wirtschaft durch Transfer von Wissen aus der Forschung in die Unternehmen des aus elf Landkreisen bestehenden ehemaligen Regierungsbezirks Lüneburg bereitgestellt. Eine der insgesamt 47 in dem EU-Großprojekt durchgeführten Maßnahmen war die Erarbeitung der Leuphana Case Studies.

Gemeinsam mit Kooperationspartnern aus dem Konvergenzgebiet wurden zwölf Case Studies zu spezifischen Herausforderungen der Region erarbeitet. Die Themenfelder sind dabei sehr unterschiedlich und reichen von Fragen des Nachhaltigkeitsmanagements, über das Veranstaltungs- und Kulturmanagement im ländlichen Raum, bis hin zu Fragen der Vernetzung von kleinen und mittelständischen Unternehmen.

Dabei wurde das Konzept der wissenschaftlichen Methode Case Study mit den Leuphana Case Studies weiterentwickelt. Diese bestehen nicht nur aus einem mehrseitigen Case-Study-Text, der dann von Studierenden bearbeitet wird. Die Leuphana Case Studies beinhalten ein didaktisches Konzept, mit dem den Bearbeiterinnen und Bearbeitern der Case Studies die Werkzeuge zur Lösung ihrer Herausforderungen vermittelt werden. So können die Case Studies von Unternehmen in vergleichbaren Situationen eingesetzt werden. Mit Hilfe des didaktischen Konzepts der Case Studies kann aus dem Wissensschatz der Mitarbeiterinnen und Mitarbeiter eines Unternehmens eine Lösung für die eigenen Herausforderungen erarbeitet werden.

Die Leuphana Case Studies sind in Zusammenarbeit mit den weiterbildenden Studiengängen der Leuphana Professional School entstanden. So wurden die didaktischen Konzepte bereits in der Praxis erprobt und darauf aufbauend weiter verfeinert. Die vorliegende Case Study spiegelt in weiten Teilen reale

Entwicklungsprozesse wider. An einigen Stellen wurden die Darstellungen didaktisch überarbeitet.

Wir wünschen Ihnen viel Erfolg und Spaß bei der Bearbeitung der vorliegenden Case Study. Wir sind uns sicher, dass Sie Werkzeuge und Fähigkeiten erlernen werden, die Ihnen bei Ihrer täglichen Arbeit und bei der Bewältigung der Herausforderungen dort helfen werden.

Christoph Kleineberg

Vorwort des Autors

Das Unternehmen jpl3, das in der Textilindustrie tätig ist, findet sich mitten in einem Shitstorm wieder. Nach einem Fernsehbericht über die Produktionsbedingungen hagelt es Kritik in den sozialen Netzwerken. Die Case Study beschäftigt sich mit den Strategien, wie das Unternehmen darauf reagieren kann und sollte. Außerdem werden Konzepte erarbeiten, mit denen das Unternehmen in Zukunft Shitstorms vorbeugen kann oder diese bereits in einem frühen Stadium beruhigen kann. Dabei wird zu Beginn das neue Kommunikationsmedium soziale Netzwerke vorgestellt. Darauf aufbauend wird eine Gefahrenanalyse durchgeführt und eine Strategie für die Krisenkommunikation erstellt. Abschließend werden Themen wie Corporate Social Responsibility behandelt.

Dr. Jörg Sikkenga

Inhaltsverzeichnis

1 **Case Study I** 1
  1.1 Vorgeschichte/Rahmenbedingungen 1
  1.2 Beschreibung der Hauptakteure 4
  1.3 Auslösung des Shitstorms 8

2 **Teaching Note** 13
  2.1 Zusammenfassung der Case Studies 13
  2.2 Lehrplan 14
    2.2.1 Thema I: Shitstorm (Definition und Systematisierung) 15
    2.2.2 Thema II: Social Media 16
    2.2.3 Thema III: Social-Media-Strategie 19
    2.2.4 Thema IV: Krisenkommunikation 20
    2.2.5 Thema V: Antwortstrategien bei Krisen/Shitstorm 22
    2.2.6 Thema VI: Issue/Issue Management 25
    2.2.7 Thema VII: Issue Management und Krisenkommunikation . 29
    2.2.8 Thema VIII: CSR 30
    2.2.9 Lehrpläne 31

3 **Anhang: Arbeitsblätter** 35

Literaturverzeichnis 39

Weiterführende Literatur 41

Abbildungsverzeichnis

Abb. 1.1 Homepage von jpl3, http://jpl3.jimdo.com/ 2
Abb. 1.2 Social-Media-Kanäle bei jpl 3 3
Abb. 1.3 Filmtitel 8
Abb. 1.4 Kinderarbeit in Bangladesch 9
Abb. 1.5 T-Shirt bei jpl 3. 10
Abb. 2.1 Social-Media-Dreieck. Quelle: nach Schmidt 2011 17
Abb. 2.2 Social-Media-Strategie Rahmenplan.Quelle: Dawson 2009. 19
Abb. 2.3 unterschiedliche Krisenarten.Quelle: Töpfer 2006. 21
Abb. 2.4 SCCT. Quelle: Thießen 2011 23
Abb. 2.5 Issue-Dreieck. 26
Abb. 2.6 Issue-Lebenszyklus. Quelle: Ingenhoff und Röttger 2006. 27
Abb. 2.7 Issue Management Prozess. Quelle: Ingenhoff und Röttger 2006 . . . 28
Abb. 2.8 Kommunikation im Krisenprozess. Quelle: Töpfer 2006 29

Tabellenverzeichnis

Tab. 2.1 Antwortstrategien bei Shitstorms 24
Tab. 2.2 Seminarplan über acht Stunden 31
Tab. 2.3 Seminarplan über mehr als 1000 Minuten 32
Tab. 3.1 Shitstorms bei anderen Unternehmen 36

Case Study I

1.1 Vorgeschichte/Rahmenbedingungen

Hauptakteur der vorliegenden Case Study ist das Bekleidungsunternehmen jpl 3[1]. Das Unternehmen wurde im Jahre 2010 von den drei Geschwistern Julius, Peter und Luisa Dreikam gegründet. Das Logo ihrer Firma (siehe Abb. 1.1) beinhaltet die Initialen sowie eine Anspielung auf den Nachnamen. Das Unternehmen hat sich spezialisiert auf den Online-Verkauf von T-Shirts.

jpl 3 verspricht seinen Kunden auf der einen Seite modische, auf der anderen Seite aber auch nachhaltige Bekleidungsstücke zu verkaufen.

So erläutert Julius Dreikam:

„Unser Ziel und unser Ansporn ist es, hippe und gleichzeitig nachhaltige Shirts zu produzieren. Um die Kosten der trendigen T-Shirts dennoch so gering und trotzdem fair zu halten, verzichten wir auf die Anmietung teurer Räumlichkeiten und bieten daher unsere Ware nur online an."

Das Unternehmen agiert somit lediglich online und ist stark im Social-Media-Bereich vertreten. So ist jpl 3 auf drei Kanälen zu finden: Homepage, Facebook sowie Twitter.

---

[1] Diese Case Study ist ein fiktionales Werk. Namen und Personen sind frei erfunden. Ereignisse und Problemstellungen sind an andere ähnliche Shitstorms angelehnt und dienen dem Zweck der universitären Lehre. Ähnlichkeiten mit realen Personen oder Schauplätzen sind rein zufällig und nicht beabsichtigt. Die dargestellten Grafiken und Texte sind urheberrechtlich geschützt. Das Textmaterial darf ohne ausdrückliche schriftliche Genehmigung der Leuphana Universität Lüneburg weder kopiert, verkauft, verliehen noch in irgendeiner anderen Form vervielfältigt und verbreitet werden.

© Springer-Verlag GmbH Deutschland 2017
J. Sikkenga, *Shitstorm-Prävention*,
DOI 10.1007/978-3-662-54016-9_1

Abb. 1.1 Homepage von jpl3, http://jpl3.jimdo.com/

Dem Nutzer/Follower stehen alle drei Kommunikationskanäle offen, was auf der Homepage entsprechend ausgewiesen ist, wie Abb. 1.2 zeigt:

jpl 3 ist im Bereich Social Media nicht nur vertreten, sondern nutzt dieses Instrument bewusst, um mit Menschen in den Dialog zu treten. So werden bei Facebook und Twitter nicht nur auf neueingetroffene T-Shirts hingewiesen, sondern auch

1.1 Vorgeschichte/Rahmenbedingungen

Abb. 1.2 Social-Media-Kanäle bei jpl 3

aktuelle Themen angestoßen, um mit den „Freunden" bei Facebook in Kontakt zu bleiben. Des Weiteren werden Gewinnspiele veranstaltet, wo von den Followern gewünscht wird, neue und kreative T-Shirts zu gestalten. Diese Art der Kommunikation kommt gut an, so dass bereits mehr als 25.000 Personen den „Gefällt mir"-Button geklickt haben und bei Twitter immerhin 5.121 Follower dem Unternehmen folgen.

Beim Herstellungsprozess der T-Shirts wird darauf geachtet, dass dieser Prozess fair verläuft. Dieser Corporate-Social-Responsibility(CSR)-Gedanke wird ebenfalls deutlich auf der Homepage:

> „jpl 3 – wir machen T-Shirts, um sich mit Mode rundum wohl zu fühlen. Unser ‚Rundum' reicht einmal um den Globus: von angesagten Trends, die wir aus Modemetropolen wie Mailand, Zagreb oder Amsterdam mitbringen bis nach Lieblingsstadt, wo wir die Reise unserer T-Shirts zu euch organisieren. Und natürlich in unsere Produktionsländer Bangladesch und Taiwan, wo wir bei unseren Partnern für faire Löhne und Arbeitsbedingungen sorgen. Denn nichts trägt sich so gut wie ein sauber hergestelltes T-Shirt.
>
> Doch wer sind eigentlich Wir? Bei uns weißt du ganz genau, wer sich um dein neues Lieblings-T-Shirt kümmert: Wir sind Julius, Peter und Luisa, drei Geschwister aus Lieblingsstadt, die Mode lieben und verschiedenste Fähigkeiten für das Modebusiness mitbringen. Wir sind aber auch Rashda, Sunita und Uma, drei unserer bengalischen Näherinnen, die für eine professionelle Verarbeitung deines neuen Lieblings-Shirts sorgen. Zu unserem Wir gehört auch die Natur: Unsere Produkte gelangen schonend und nachhaltig ohne unnötige Umweltbelastung, aus Asien nach Deutschland. jpl 3 – unsere Shirt-Stories haben ein Happy End."

1.2 Beschreibung der Hauptakteure

Zur Darstellung der Gründer und Geschäftsführer liest man auf der Homepage Folgendes:

1.2 Beschreibung der Hauptakteure

Julius Dreikam:

Julius ist der Älteste der drei Geschwister und hat Economic Studies in Köln und Singapur studiert. Während seiner Studienzeit in Singapur hat er sein Herz an den Kontinent verschenkt und möchte die asiatische Kreativität mit ostfriesischen Handelsmethoden kombinieren. Sein Style ist klassisch, darf aber auch mal eine verrückte Note haben. Dazu kombiniert er gern knallige Shirts seines eigenen Labels mit lässigen Sakkos.

Luisa Dreikam:

Den weiblichen Part im Unternehmen stellt Luisa. Sie hat Modemanagement an der Hochschule für Textilwirtschaft in München studiert und sitzt gern selbst an der Nähmaschine und denkt über neue Looks nach. Sie freut sich über transparente Elemente in ihren Entwürfen – und über Transparenz im Unternehmen.

1.2 Beschreibung der Hauptakteure

Peter Dreikam:

Mit Peter wird das Trio komplettiert: Er ist ein wahres Logistiktalent und hat BWL und Transportwesen in Hamburg studiert. Aber schon früher lag die Organisation der Familienurlaube in seiner Hand. Er kontrolliert, wie das T-Shirt vom Entwurf bis zum neuen Lieblingsteil wird – und steht dabei immer mit den Produktionsländern in Kontakt, damit Stoffe und Produktionsbedingungen sauber bleiben.

1.3 Auslösung des Shitstorms

Der Fernsehsender 3sat zeigt eine Reportage mit dem Titel „Die Preis-Lüge: Wer zahlt für mein T-Shirt"[2] (Abb. 1.3) über die Lebens- und Arbeitsbedingungen von Näherinnen in der Textilindustrie, die ihren Alltag dokumentieren.

Zu den Verhältnissen heißt es im Bericht:

„In dieser Großfabrik wird im Akkord für westliche Handelsketten genäht. […] Eine Näherin muss bis zu 250 T-Shirts pro Stunde bearbeiten und verdient rund einen Euro pro Tag. Der Preisdruck der Handelsketten ließe nicht mehr zu."

Die Expertin, Dr. Bettina Musiolek, Mitarbeiterin im Entwicklungspolitischen Netzwerk, berichtet:

„In Asien gibt es eine Allianz von Arbeitsrechtsorganisationen, die Asia Floor Wage Campaign, die haben für die Näherinnen ausgerechnet, wie hoch müsste ein Lohn zum Leben sein. Der Unterschied zwischen dem tatsächlichen Lohn der Näherinnen und einem Lohn zum Leben in Bangladesch ist 1 zu 6."

Abb. 1.3 Filmtitel

---

[2] Hier abrufbar: https://www.youtube.com/watch?v=w6Njw0YDuF8

1.3 Auslösung des Shitstorms

Abb. 1.4 Kinderarbeit in Bangladesch

Im Laufe der Reportage stellt sich heraus, dass jpl 3 ebenfalls in der gezeigten Näherei produzieren lässt. Die Abb. 1.4 zeigt Kinder, die T-Shirts einpacken und die Abb. 1.5 zeigt eines dieser T-Shirts auf der Homepage von jpl 3:

Im Bericht heißt es dazu: „Selbst Unternehmen wie jpl 3, die sich eine nachhaltige Produktion auf die Fahne geschrieben haben, lassen hier produzieren."

Zeitgleich sitzen in Lieblingsstadt die drei Firmengründer zusammen und besprechen ihren Kommunikationsetat und den Media-Plan für das folgende Geschäftsjahr. Plötzlich platzt die Assistentin der Geschäftsführung, Meike B., in die Besprechung mit folgenden Worten: „Leute, das müsst ihr euch angucken. Da könnten Probleme auf uns zukommen", schaltet den Fernseher an und gezeigt wird noch der Abspann der Dokumentation. Unklar, worauf die ansonsten immer sehr zurückhaltende Assistentin hinausmöchte, reagiert Julius ein wenig ungehalten: „Meike, was soll der Scheiß? Wir sind hier mitten in einem wichtigen Meeting und du willst mit uns Fernsehen gucken?" Schnell reagiert Meike und ruft die Mediathek von 3sat auf und lässt die wichtigsten Szenen sowie die Erwähnung des Unternehmens jpl 3 noch einmal ablaufen.

JPL3 T-Shirt Shop

Start   Ladies   Jungs   Über Uns   CSR   Kontakt

T-Shirts für Jungs

Unser Klassiker

Dieses schlichte T-Shirt besticht durch seinen Tragekomfort und die außergewöhnliche Farbe, mit der du der Hingucker auf jeder Party bist.

White   30,00 €

30,00 €

Abb. 1.5 T-Shirt bei jpl 3

Folgender Dialog läuft im Anschluss an das Gezeigte:

Luisa: „Danke Meike, dass du so schnell reagiert hast."
Julius: „Ja, danke und ´tschuldige, dass ich gerade so reagiert habe."
Meike: „Bereits vergessen. Ich gehe dann mal."
Julius: „Peter, was ist an diesem Bericht wahr?"
Peter: „Ich weiß es nicht. Ich weiß es wirklich nicht. Ich kann es mir nicht erklären."
Luisa: „F***, F****, F****, das darf doch nicht wahr sein. Wir wollen uns doch gerade von diesen Unternehmen abgrenzen und fair produzieren und … "
Julius: „Ja, dann so etwas."
Peter: „Ich kann mir das wirklich nicht erklären."
Julius: „Peter, das ist ein Fehler, der einfach nicht passieren darf. Aber darum können wir uns jetzt erst einmal nicht kümmern. Dieser Fehler kann unser gesamtes Geschäft kaputt machen. Wir müssen nun so schnell wie möglich darauf reagieren. Ansonsten schwappt ein Shitstorm über uns, der sich gewaschen hat. Vorschläge?"

1.3 Auslösung des Shitstorms

Derweil in einem anderen Teil der Republik:
Anna P. sitzt vor ihrem Fernseher und schaut sich die Reportage an. Anna P. ist empört über das Geschäftsgebaren von jpl 3. Sie selbst war bis jetzt begeisterte Kundin von jpl 3. Begeistert, weil die T-Shirts wunderbar aussehen, eine sehr gute Qualität haben und man sie mit gutem Gewissen tragen kann, da die Näherinnen gut bezahlt werden. Doch mit dem Fernsehbeitrag ändert sich die Haltung von Anna. Sie ist einfach nur noch sauer auf jpl 3. Mit einer gehörigen Portion Wut im Bauch geht sie an ihren Laptop und postet als Erste auf der Facebook-Seite von jpl 3 den Fernsehbeitrag und folgende Nachricht: „Liebes jpl 3-Team ... nee, das war einmal. Ich habe Euch bislang vertraut. Da sprecht Ihr von fairem Produzieren und dann so etwas. Ich bin stinksauer auf Euch. Ihr seid leider wie alle anderen auch. Hauptsache, der Profit stimmt. Mich habt ihr als Kundin verloren."

Innerhalb weniger Stunden gehen auf der Facebook-Seite hunderte Posts und auf der Twitter-Seite hunderte Tweets ein, die sich über das Geschäftsgebaren des Bekleidungsunternehmens beschweren. Dabei gehen die Aktionen auf Facebook über das Liken von Posts (insbesondere von Anna P.) über Kommentare mit kurzen, aber wertenden Aussagen (z. B. Schweine, big dislike, ihr sollt euch schämen, ...) hin zu Posts, die längere Aussagen tätigen und eine besondere moralische Schuld von jpl 3 herausstellen.

Wie kann jpl 3 reagieren?

Teaching Note 2

Die vorliegenden Case Studies sind als Kombination der beiden Typen Case Study und Case Problem Method konzipiert (vgl. Kaiser 1983). Der Fokus hängt von der genutzten Länge des Falles ab.

Die Case Study I legt den Fokus auf das Erkennen des Problems und Ziel ist es, Lösungsalternativen und die zu treffende Entscheidung zu erarbeiten. Die Case Study II wiederum setzt den Schwerpunkt auf eine kritische Reflexion der in der Case Study vorgestellten Lösungsansätze sowie die Ermittlung alternativer Lösungsansätze.

Die Teaching Note umfasst verschiedene Abschnitte:

In Abschnitt I werden die Case Studies noch einmal kurz dargestellt, wodurch dem Lehrenden die Möglichkeit gegeben wird, den Teilnehmern die Case Study kurz bekannt und Lust auf sie zu machen.

In Abschnitt II werden verschiedene Themenbausteine vorgestellt, die sich je nach Dauer der Veranstaltung zusammenstellen lassen. So ergeben sich drei verschiedene Lehrpläne, die am Ende des Abschnitts vorgestellt werden.

Abschnitt III umfasst die verwendete und weiterführende Literatur.

Um die Case Study noch besser didaktisch nutzen zu können, werden in Abschn. 4 Arbeitsblätter bereitgestellt.

2.1 Zusammenfassung der Case Studies

Die vorliegende Lehr- und Lernfallstudie „Shitstorm" liefert eine komplexe Situation:

Ein junges Unternehmen, jpl 3, welches sich der Nachhaltigkeit verschrieben hat, verkauft lediglich T-Shirts online. Die drei jungen Gründer und Geschwister der Firma haben sich bewusst für die reine Online-Kommunikation entschieden und sind daher auf drei Kanälen zu finden: Homepage, Facebook sowie Twitter. Das Unternehmen stellt auf allen Kanälen heraus, dass es nachhaltig produziert und sucht den Dialog mit den Kunden.

Im Rahmen eines Fernsehbeitrags über die Arbeits- und Lebensbedingungen von Näherinnen wird ein T-Shirt gezeigt, welches von jpl 3 ebenfalls verkauft wird. Die gezeigten Aufnahmen stehen in einem klaren Widerspruch (z. B. Unterbezahlung der Näherinnen, Kinderarbeit) zu den Vorsätzen der Gründer von jpl 3.

Aufgrund dieses Beitrags erscheinen in kurzer Zeit eine Menge negativer Posts und Tweets auf den jeweiligen Kanälen.

In der erweiterten Fassung der Case Study (Case Study II) erweitert sich der Fall um eine Entschuldigungsstrategie mitsamt der Bildung einer Task-Force, die den Fall genau untersuchen möchte. Darüber hinaus wird ein Video erstellt, was dazu dienen soll, das Vertrauen der Konsumenten zurückzugewinnen. Dieses Video ist jedoch so überzeichnet, dass es von (potenziellen) Kunden als Greenwashing wahrgenommen wird und somit ein erneuter Shitstorm losbricht.

2.2 Lehrplan

Mittels der vorliegenden Case Study sollen folgende Fragen im Laufe der jeweiligen Lehrveranstaltung beantwortet werden:

- Was sind Shitstorms?
- Gibt es verschiedene Arten von Shitstorms?
- Wie begegnet man Shitstorms aus Unternehmenssicht?
- Welche Antwortstrategien existieren im Rahmen einer Krisenkommunikation?
- Was macht Social Media aus?
- Wie sieht eine Social-Media-Strategie aus?
- Wie können Unternehmen präventiv einem Shitstorm begegnen?
- Wie gehen Unternehmen mit dem Themenfeld Corporate Social Responsibility (CSR) um?

Somit werden folgende, grundlegende Themen behandelt:

- Shitstorm (Definition und Systematisierung)
- Social Media
- Social-Media-Strategie
- Krisenkommunikation

2.2 Lehrplan

- Antwortstrategien bei Krisen/Shitstorm
- Issue Management
- Zusammenspiel zwischen Issue Management und Krisenkommunikation
- CSR

2.2.1 Thema I: Shitstorm (Definition und Systematisierung)

Die Anzahl an wissenschaftlichen Publikationen zur Shitstormthematik ist gering, so dass auch die Anzahl an Definitionen laut jetzigem Kenntnisstand des Autors überschaubar ist.

Den Begriff „Shitstorm" prägte in Deutschland der bekannte Blogger Sascha Lobo. Er (Lobo 2010) definiert das Phänomen wie folgt: „In kurzer Zeit wird online eine Vielzahl an kritischen Aussagen getätigt, die aggressiv, beleidigend oder bedrohend sind".

Der Begriff „Shitstorm" ist ein rein deutscher Ausdruck. Im englischen Sprachgebrauch ist die Rede von einem „Online firestorm" oder einer „social media crisis bzw. paracrisis". So definiert Pfeffer et al. (2014) den Begriff "Online firestorm" als "sudden discharge of large quantities of messages containing negative WOM and complaint behavior against a person, company or group in social media networks".

Eine vage Definition von social media crisis liefert Coombs (2014):

„A social media crisis is a situation that emergence in or is amplified by social media. Unfortunately that is very vague definition that even people who helped to popularize the term now find does not work well at all. Social media crisis essentially are risks that an organization is managing in public view. These risks look like crisis and often demand a communicative response. These situations have been called paracrisis because the situation is like a crisis but is actually a form of risk management."

Himmelreich und Einwiller (2015) verwenden in ihrem Überblicksartikel zu diesem Thema beide oben genannten Definitionen und kommen zu folgendem Schluss:

„Zusammenfassend ist unter einem Shitstorm hier eine Situation zu verstehen, in der sich innerhalb kurzer Zeit in den unterschiedlichsten Anwendungen des Social Webs eine große Menge an kritischen Kommentaren über eine Organisation oder Person verbreitet, wodurch die Reputation des angegriffenen Objekts gefährdet wird."

In dieser Definition werden bereits verschiedene Themen wie Social Media und Reputation angesprochen, denen sich in anderen Kapiteln gewidmet wird.

Coombs (2014) stellt vier verschiedene Arten von Social-Media-Krisen bzw. Parakrisen dar, die sich hinsichtlich des Auslösers des Shitstorms unterscheiden:

- Fehlnutzung von Social-Media-Kanälen: Hierbei handelt es sich um einen Fehler auf Seiten des Unternehmens. Die Fehler können verschiedentlicher Natur sein, wie z. B. die Nutzung eines falschen Fotos oder ein falscher Hashtag.

Bei den anderen Arten des Shitstorms sind die Posts von Usern der Auslöser für einen Shitstorm.

- Unzufriedenheit von Kunden: Bei dieser Art des Shitstorms machen Kunden ihrer Unzufriedenheit Luft und posten dieses in sozialen Netzwerken. Problem für das Unternehmen besteht dann, wenn ebenfalls unzufriedene Kunden sich daran beteiligen.
- Hass von Kunden: Hier posten Personen aus Hass gegenüber dem Unternehmen etwas. Der Hass kann dabei vielfältiger Natur sein (ehemalige Mitarbeiter, enttäuschte Kunden).
- Die vierte und letzte Art von Shitstorms bezeichnet Coombs als Herausforderungen für das Unternehmen, die sich Social Issues stellen müssen. Dem Thema Issues wird sich im Abschnitt VI gewidmet.

2.2.2 Thema II: Social Media

Was deutlich wird, ist, dass das Phänomen Shitstorm im Bereich Social Media verankert ist. Was macht Social Media aber aus?

Eine oftmals zitierte Quelle von Kaplan und Haenlein (2010) definiert Social Media wie folgt: „Social Media is a group of internet-based applications that build on the ideological and technological foundations of Web 2.0, and that allow the creation and exchange of User Generated Content". Der Fokus liegt hier auf dem technischen Hintergrund des Web 2.0, das es jedem ermöglicht, Inhalte zu erschaffen und mit anderen auszutauschen.

Mark Schaeffer (2010) beschreibt das Phänomen Social Media mit den drei Schlagwörtern evolution, revolution und contribution.

Social Media stellt eine neue Kommunikationsart dar, die eine neue **Evolut**ionsstufe der Kommunikation ist. Sie dient sowohl der Interaktion als auch dem Austausch. Damit stellt es eine Erweiterung anderer Kommunikationsarten für Unternehmen dar wie z. B. Radio oder Fernsehen. Die Interaktionsmöglichkeiten

2.2 Lehrplan

sind hier sehr gering ausgeprägt. Des Weiteren mutet die Social-Media-Kommunikation eine Form der Face-to-Face-Kommunikation an, findet jedoch im semiöffentlichen Raum statt.

Social Media ist durch die technische Grundlage des Internets nahezu weltweit zugänglich und verfügbar. Durch diese **Revolution** besitzt Social Media eine enorme Reichweite im Vergleich zu klassischen Medien. Des Weiteren ist diese digitale Echtzeit-Kommunikation deutlich aktueller und reaktionsschneller als klassische Medien.

Zentraler Bestandteil von Social Media ist, dass normale Menschen die Veröffentlicher sind (**contribution**). Dieses Phänomen, welches als User-generated Content bezeichnet wird, ist zentraler Bestandteil von Social Media und wird bereits in der oben genannten Definition von Kaplan und Haenlein deutlich.

Eine Systematik der unzähligen Social-Media-Anwendungen liefert Schmidt (2011) mit seinem Social-Media-Dreieck, wie Abbildung Abb. 2.1 verdeutlicht:

So unterscheidet Schmidt drei Anwendungen, die jeweils unterschiedliche Fokusse besitzen.

Der erste Fokus umfasst Anwendungen, die darauf abzielen, bestehende Beziehungen zu pflegen, aber auch neue Beziehungen zu knüpfen. Hierbei gibt es noch die Unterscheidung der Beziehungen in privater und beruflicher Natur.

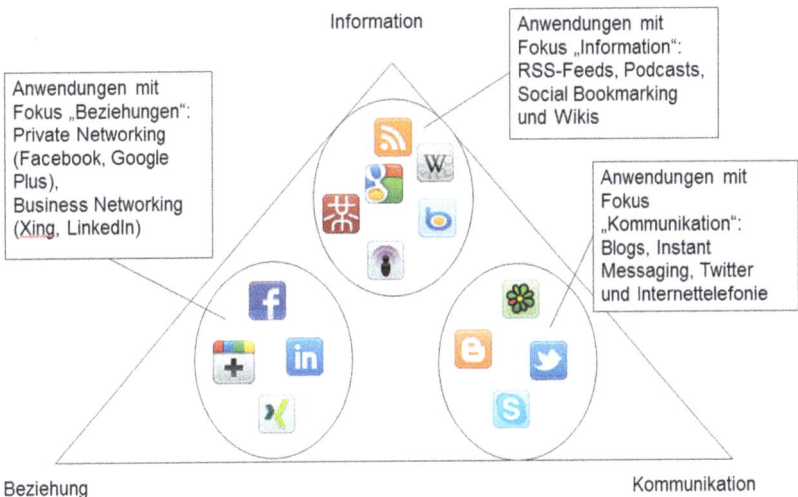

Abb. 2.1 Social-Media-Dreieck. Quelle: nach Schmidt 2011

Der zweite Fokus der Anwendungen umfasst den Aspekt der Information. Das Ziel dieser Anwendungen ist es, sowohl Informationen zu sammeln als auch diese zu teilen.

Der dritte und letzte Schwerpunkt bei den Anwendungen im Bereich Social Media liegt auf dem Fokus der Kommunikation. Diese Anwendungen dienen dazu, zwei oder mehrere Nutzer miteinander in Kontakt treten zu lassen, damit diese sich unterhalten können. Dies kann sowohl in Echtzeit geschehen, mit oder ohne visueller Unterstützung (Möglichkeit der Videotelefonie mittels Skype), oder zeitlich versetzt.

Was bedeutet dies aber nun für den Shitstorm:
Dazu der Medienwissenschaftler Pörksen (2015) in einem Interview mit der dpa:

> Pörksen: „Die Debatte der vergangenen Tage zeigt, dass es im Grunde genommen einen verborgenen Kulturkampf gibt zwischen den vernetzten Vielen, die im Netz protestieren, und denjenigen, die sich in den klassischen Medien artikulieren.
> dpa: Was meinen Sie mit Kulturkampf?
> Pörksen: Nun, wir befinden uns in einem bedeutsamen Moment des Medienwandels – auf dem Weg von der Mediendemokratie der klassischen Leitmedien hin zu Empörungsdemokratie des digitalen Zeitalters. Hier verlieren die traditionellen Machtzentren und publizistischen Monopole an Einfluss. Und auf einmal kann sich jeder zuschalten. Und am Ende des Tages empören sich schließlich alle wechselseitig – eben über die Empörung der jeweils anderen Seite. Genau so ist es passiert.
> dpa: Wenn ich Sie richtig verstehe, raten Sie dazu, bei einem Shitstorm die Beleidigungen in Gedanken wegzustreichen und zu ergründen, welches gesellschaftliche Thema dahintersteht?
> Pörksen: Ganz genau. Man denke nur an einen Shitstorm, der sich gegen ein Unternehmen richtet: Hier zeigen sich oft brisante, manchmal einfach berechtigte, in jedem Fall ökonomisch hochrelevante Wertkonzepte von Konsumenten und Kunden. Man will kein Greenwashing, man möchte keine Heuchelei, man ist gegen ungerechte Arbeitsbedingungen. Das alles mag dann scharf und übermäßig aggressiv formuliert sein. Und doch: Wir brauchen für den gesellschaftlichen Dialog die Figur des Shitstorm-Interpreten, der die Frage stellt: Was steckt dahinter? Welchen aufklärerischen Sinn hat die scheinbar sinnlose Empörung?

Pörksen macht also darauf aufmerksam, dass die Kommunikation sich gewandelt hat. Nicht mehr die klassischen Medien bestimmen die Agenda, sondern es sind zunehmend die Konsumenten und normalen User. Himmelreich und Einwiller (2015) beschäftigen sich mit der Thematik der Diffusion der online geäußerten

2.2 Lehrplan

Kritik nicht-professioneller Internetnutzer in die traditionelle Medienberichterstattung ausführlicher.

2.2.3 Thema III: Social-Media-Strategie

Bevor sich dem Thema „Shitstorm" weiter genähert wird, soll sich dem Thema Social-Media-Kommunikation für Unternehmen genähert werden. Es ist unerlässlich, eine Social-Media-Strategie für den Auftritt des Unternehmens in sozialen Medien zu entwickeln.

Eine Social-Media-Strategie (Abb. 2.2) umfasst nach Dawson (2009) sowohl eine Innen- wie auch eine Außenperspektive.

Bevor eine Strategie verfasst wird, sollte man als Unternehmen sich erst einmal die Frage stellen, ob die Nutzung von Social Media für das Unternehmen einen Mehrwert bietet und sich daher wirtschaftlich lohnt. Oftmals wird Social Media genutzt, weil es alle machen. Falls diese Frage mit ja beantwortet wird, steht eine

Abb. 2.2 Social-Media-Strategie Rahmenplan.Quelle: Dawson 2009

Beobachtung der Nutzung der sozialen Medien allgemein und von seinen unmittelbaren Konkurrenten an, ebenso wie die Vertrautmachung mit Monitoring Tools. In der Innenperspektive müssen Ziele festgelegt werden, die mit Hilfe der Nutzung von Social Media erreicht werden sollen. Dieses müssen schriftlich fixiert werden. Anschließend müssen die Mitarbeiter aufgeklärt werden, welche Chancen und Risiken sich bei der Nutzung von Social Media ergeben können. Dies betrifft nicht nur den Social-Media-Kanal des Unternehmens, sondern auch die private Nutzung, falls Rückschlüsse auf das Unternehmen gezogen werden können. Daher sollte man hier frühzeitig die Mitarbeiter schulen und sogenannte Social Media Guidelines entwickeln. Des Weiteren sollte man Strategien erarbeiten, wie man auf bestimmte Dinge reagiert und entsprechende Maßnahmen treffen. Nachdem die Ziele bestimmt wurden, kann daraus eine Strategie abgeleitet werden, die entsprechende Aktivitäten und Verantwortliche vorsieht. Die Außenperspektive spiegelt das Engagement gemäß der Strategie des Unternehmens wider. Um das Kommunikationsinstrument optimal zu nutzen, sollte das Unternehmen auch in einen wirklichen Dialog mit den Nutzern treten. Dies bedeutet, dass Social Media nicht als reines Marketing-Instrument mit dem Posten neuer Produkte und Dienstleistungen benutzt wird, sondern als ein Medium, welches in den Dialog tritt mit den Nutzern, um diese kennenzulernen.

Weitere Themenfelder in diesem Bereich können sein:

- Erfolgsgeschichten von Facebook
- Social Media Guidelines
- Erfolgreiche Posts bei Facebook

2.2.4 Thema IV: Krisenkommunikation

Ein Shitstorm stellt eine besondere Form der Krisenkommunikation dar.
Töpfer (2006) definiert Krise wie folgt:

> „Eine Krise lässt sich generell als ein eingetretenes Risiko definieren, das vorher bereits erkannt und bewertet oder auch überhaupt nicht wahrgenommen wurde und damit völlig überraschend eintrat".

Damit spricht Töpfer bei einer Krise von einem Risikofall, dessen Eintrittsfall mit einer Wahrscheinlichkeit kalkuliert werden kann.
Charakteristika einer Krise sind laut Töpfer (2006) folgende Elemente: Es handelt sich um eine öffentliche Angelegenheit, die eine vorübergehende Existenzgefährdung des Unternehmens bedeutet. Darüber hinaus ist der Ausgang einer

2.2 Lehrplan

Krise uneindeutig. Damit einher geht die Gefährdung von Unternehmenszielen. Eine Krise weist einen Prozesscharakter auf und die Steuerung einer Krise ist ungewiss und aufgrund ihrer Dynamik birgt sie eine gewisse Unkontrollierbarkeit. Es lassen sich verschiedene Risikoarten identifizieren, z. B. die Ertrags- und die plötzliche Unternehmenskrise, wie Abb. 2.3 zeigt:

Bei einer Ertragskrise handelt es sich um eine schleichende Krise, die sich langsam entwickelt und ein öffentliches Interesse besteht am Anfang dieser Art von Krise kaum. Bei der Ertragskrise handelt es sich um eine strategische Krise, wo das Unternehmen eine falsche Strategie verfolgt, die erst langsam wahrgenommen wird. Die strategische Krise führt zu einer Erfolgskrise und damit im Laufe der Zeit auch zu einer Liquiditätskrise. Ein Beispiel für eine Ertragskrise wäre eine Bank, die eine Strategie verfolgt, die sich jedoch als falsch herausstellt. Dies führt zu einer Gewinnwarnung und einer Ankündigung der Streichung von Jobs. Dadurch entwickeln sich ein öffentliches Interesse und eine Vielzahl an Demonstrationen gegen diese Streichung. Je nach Qualität des Krisenmanagements steigt bzw. sinkt das öffentliche Interesse und damit auch die Anzahl an Medienberichterstattungen.

Bei einer plötzlichen Unternehmenskrise hingegen sieht sich das Unternehmen ohne Vorwarnungen dieser Krise gegenüber. Dabei ist das öffentliche Interesse

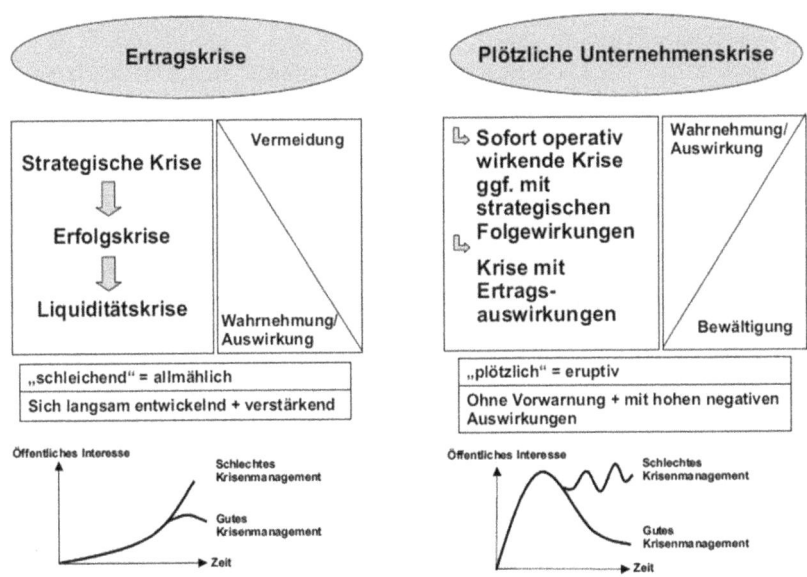

Abb. 2.3 unterschiedliche Krisenarten. Quelle: Töpfer 2006

groß und es kommt auf das Krisenmanagement an, ob das öffentliche Interesse zu- oder abnimmt.

Ein Shitstorm lässt sich je nach Ursache beiden Krisenarten zuordnen. Auf den ersten Blick erscheint ein Shitstorm als eine plötzliche Unternehmenskrise. Allerdings erweist sich die Shitstorm-Art Herausforderung als ein Zusammenspiel der beiden oben dargestellten Krisenarten. Auf der einen Seite ist es beim Ausbruch eine plötzliche Unternehmenskrise. Da es sich hierbei jedoch bei den Auslösern um „Social Issues" handelt, die, wie im folgenden Abschnitt dargestellt wird, von den Unternehmen bearbeitet und gesteuert werden können, lässt sich diese Art des Shitstorms auch der Ertragskrise zuordnen aufgrund einer unzureichenden Strategie bzw. fehlenden Prävention bei der Identifizierung des Issues und einer entsprechenden Ausarbeitung einer Strategie.

2.2.5 Thema V: Antwortstrategien bei Krisen/Shitstorm

Bei Krisen jeglicher Art steht für das Unternehmen vor allem die eigene Reputation auf dem Spiel. So muss daher Ziel jeglicher Kommunikation sein, die positive Reputation aufrechtzuerhalten.

Reputation kann als Summe der bewerteten Wahrnehmung einer Organisation durch eigene oder die Erfahrung Dritter definiert werden (vgl. Thießen 2011, Argenti und Druckenmiller 2004).

Mit dem Themenfeld der Reputation und der Aufrechthaltung im Rahmen von Krisen hat sich insbesondere Coombs im Rahmen seiner Situational Crisis Communication Theory (SCCT) beschäftigt.

Die SCCT wurde von Coombs und Holladay 1996 entwickelt und durch Ergebnisse empirischer Forschungen weiterentwickelt (Coombs 2004, 2006, 2007, 2007, 2010). Sie geht von zwei Annahmen aus (vgl. auch Thießen 2011): Krisen werden von Stakeholdern unterschiedlich wahrgenommen. Diese Wahrnehmung hängt von der zugeschriebenen Krisenschuld ab. Entsprechend wirkt sich dies auf die Reputation vom Unternehmen aus.

Bei der SCCT, siehe Abb. 2.4, handelt es sich um ein Prozessmodell mit zwei Schritten. Im ersten Schritt ist die Krisenverantwortlichkeit des Unternehmens zu bestimmen. Je stärker die Stakeholder die Verantwortlichkeit dem Unternehmen zuschreiben, desto größer der mögliche negative Effekt auf die Reputation des Unternehmens. Die Zuschreibung ist jedoch von weiteren Faktoren abhängig, die bestimmt werden müssen. So hängt die Zuschreibung der Stakeholder davon ab, ob das Unternehmen bereits vorher in Krisen verwickelt war. Hier findet die Attribution nach dem Motto „wer einmal lügt, dem glaubt man nicht" statt. Ebenso einen

2.2 Lehrplan

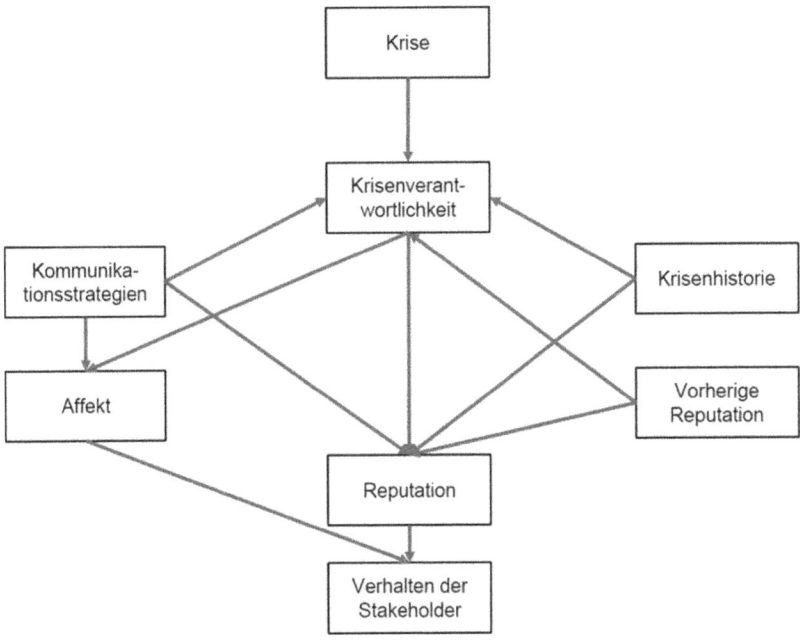

Abb. 2.4 SCCT. Quelle: Thießen 2011

Einfluss hat die Reputation des Unternehmens vor der Krise. Die Verantwortlichkeitszuschreibung für die Krise ist höher, desto geringer die Reputation ist. Auch auf der Verhaltensebene macht sich die Zuschreibung bemerkbar. So führt eine Verantwortlichkeitszuschreibung zu einem negativen Weiterempfehlungsverhalten und einem reduzierten Kaufverhalten, ausgelöst durch Zorn und Ärger.

Durch ein strategisches Kommunikationsverhalten ist es nun möglich, sowohl das Verhalten der Stakeholder als auch die Zuschreibung von Reputation zu beeinflussen.

Als generelle Antwortstrategien bei Krisen schlägt Coombs (2007) im Rahmen seiner Situational Crisis Communication Theory Folgende vor:

- Leugnende Antwortstrategien
  - Ankläger angreifen
  - Leugnen
  - Sündenbock suchen

- Abschwächende Antwortstrategien
  - Rausreden
  - Verharmlosen
- Wiederherstellende Antwortstrategien
  - Entschädigen
  - Entschuldigen
- Unterstützende Antwortstrategien
  - Erinnern an das Gute
  - Einschmeicheln
  - Opferrolle

Für den Krisenfall „Shitstorm" schlägt Coombs (2014) die in Tab. 2.1 aufgelisteten Strategien vor:
Bei einer Fehlnutzung von Seiten des Unternehmens reicht eine Entschuldigung meistens aus. Ist der Kunde unzufrieden und macht diese publik, sollte das Unternehmen das Problem, welches zur Unzufriedenheit geführt hat, lösen. Dazu gehören das Entschuldigen und das Entschädigen des Kunden, indem dieser z. B. ein neues Produkt erhält. Des Weiteren sollte man den Kunden an die bislang gute Zusammenarbeit erinnern und sich wünschen, dass diese Zusammenarbeit nach wie vor Bestand hat.

Tab. 2.1 Antwortstrategien bei Shitstorms

	Fehlnutzung	Kundenunzufriedenheit	Hass	Herausforderung
Ankläger angreifen				
Leugnen				
Sündenbock suchen				
Rausreden				
Verharmlosen				
Entschädigen		X		
Entschuldigen	X	X		
Erinnern an das Gute		X		
Einschmeicheln				
Opferrolle				

Matrix Antwortstrategien bei Shitstorms

2.2 Lehrplan

Bei einem Shitstorm, welcher durch Hass hervorgerufen wird, schlägt Coombs vor, ihn auszusitzen. Bei der Shitstorm-Art Herausforderung gibt es keine festgelegte Strategie, da dieses im Einzelfall zu entscheiden ist.

Im Rahmen der Case Study II wird deutlich, dass beim ersten Shitstorm von Seiten jpl 3 versucht wird, die Verantwortlichkeit für die Krise jemand anderem zuzuschreiben. Daneben finden auch Antwortstrategien, wie wiederherstellende und unterstützende Antwortstrategien Anwendung.

Beim zweiten Shitstorm, der aufgrund von jpl 3 produzierten Videos ausgelöst wird, liegt die Verantwortung für die Krise bei jpl 3. Verschiedene Antwortstrategien sind hier denkbar und sollen im Rahmen der Bearbeitung aufgezeigt werden.

2.2.6 Thema VI: Issue/Issue Management

Um einer Krise präventiv entgegenzuwirken, bietet sich ein Issue Management an. Zunächst soll aber das Thema „Issue" behandelt werden, um dann das Issue Management näher zu beschreiben.

Ingenhoff und Röttger (2006) definieren Issues wie folgt:

> „Als Issues werden Themen verstanden, die die Organisation tatsächlich oder potenziell betreffen (Relevanz), mit unterschiedlichen Ansprüchen auf Seiten der Stakeholder und der Organisation belegt sind (Erwartungslücke) und unterschiedlich interpretiert werden können, Konfliktpotenzial aufweisen (Konflikt) und von öffentlichem Interesse (Öffentlichkeit) sind."

Das Aufkommen und die Entwicklung von Issues werden vor allem durch drei Handlungs- und Einstellungssysteme (siehe Abb. 2.5) beeinflusst, die aufgrund unterschiedlicher Interessenslagen in Konflikt geraten.

So ist es zunächst das Unternehmen selbst. Dieses hat neben dem Oberziel der Gewinnmaximierung Unterziele formuliert, die diesem Oberziel förderlich sind oder dieses einschränken. (Bsp: die Meyer-Werft produziert Kreuzfahrschiffe und diese müssen auf der Ems Richtung Nordsee gefahren werden. Diese Kreuzfahrschiffe werden aber immer größer, so dass Schwierigkeiten in absehbarer Zeit auf das Unternehmen zukommen, wenn die Ems nicht den Anforderungen der Schiffe entspricht). Des Weiteren existiert die Meinung der Anspruchsgruppen. Die haben bestimmte Erwartungen an das Unternehmen. (So erwarten die Mitarbeiter, dass das Unternehmen ihren Standort nicht wechselt und weiterhin in Papenburg ihre Schiffe baut. Die Anwohner der Ems wollen nicht, dass die Ems vertieft wird, da so erheblich in das Ökosystem eingegriffen werden und dieses zu Problemen führen würde). Diese jeweiligen Vorstellungen treffen nun auf die öffentliche Meinung,

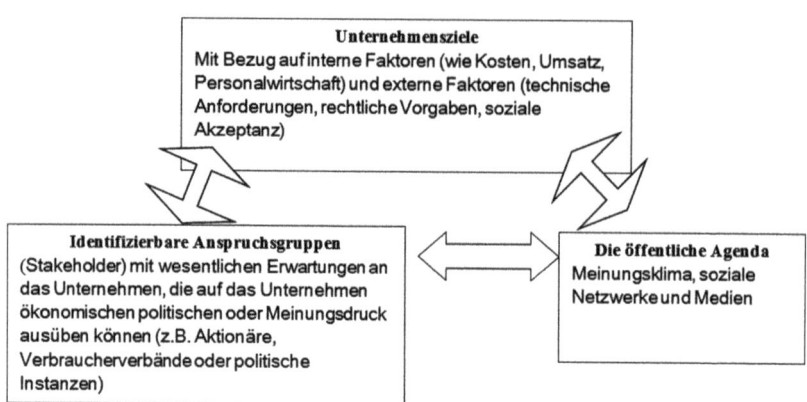

Abb. 2.5 Issue-Dreieck

auf die öffentliche Agenda. Aus diesen drei Vorstellungen entwickelt sich dann, je nach den unterschiedlichen Kräfteverhältnissen, das wirkliche Vorgehen. (Die öffentliche Meinung, die Politiker und die Medien vertraten ebenfalls die Ansicht, dass eine Emsvertiefung nicht in Betracht gezogen werden könnte. Man entschied sich daher für den Bau eines Sperrwerks, wobei ausdrücklich betont wurde, dass die Meyer-Werft bei den Planungen keine Bedeutung hatte.)

Ein Issue durchläuft verschiedene Phasen, dem sogenannten Issue-Lebenszyklus. Die einzelnen Phasen des Issue-Lebenszyklus sind gekennzeichnet durch ein zunehmendes Interesse der Betroffenen und eine zunehmende Formalisierung. Die Einflussmöglichkeiten des Unternehmens sinken jedoch dementsprechend.

Der Issue-Lebenszyklus (Abb. 2.6) folgt einer immanenten Interaktions- und Entwicklungslogik, die jedes systematische Issue-Prozess-Management zwangsläufig selbst bestimmt.

Latenzphase: In der Latenzphase ist der Druck der Öffentlichkeit kaum gegeben, da das Problem noch undefiniert ist und unbemerkt von Seiten der Öffentlichkeit vorhanden ist. Um bereits in dieser frühen Phase Issues durch das Unternehmen zu identifizieren, stehen folgende, beispielhafte Techniken zur Verfügung:

- Trend-Extrapolation
- Scanning und Monitoring
- Diffusionstheorie
- Delphi-Methode
- Szenario-Technik

2.2 Lehrplan

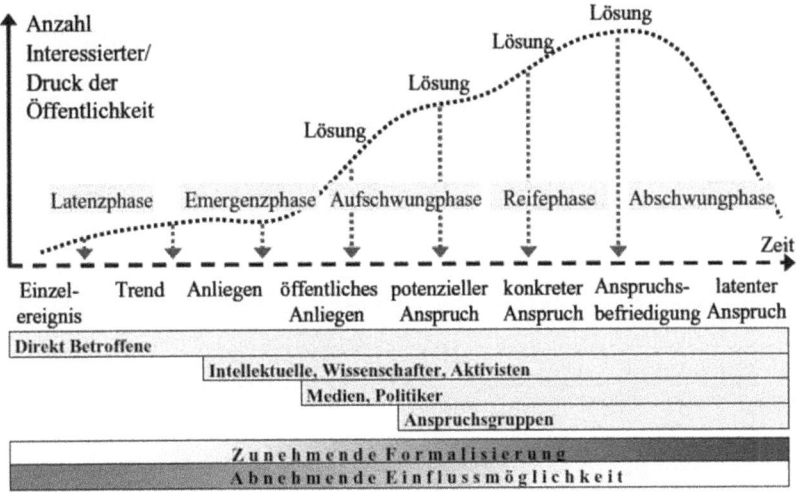

Abb. 2.6 Issue-Lebenszyklus. Quelle: Ingenhoff und Röttger 2006

Die Issues werden dabei anhand von bestimmten Kriterien, wie z. B. nach der Bedrohung der Unternehmensziele, ausgewählt.

Emergenzphase: Kennzeichen dieser Phase ist es, dass das Problem erkannt und definiert wird. Es findet somit eine Konkretisierung des Problems statt. Hier treten die ersten Experten auf, die Ursachen und Natur des Problems diskutieren und erste Lösungsalternativen aufstellen. Dieses findet unter dem Aspekt der Implementierung und gezielter kommunikativen Strategien statt.

Die Organisation muss sich der wichtigen Instrumente der Medienarbeit und gesellschaftsbezogener Aktivitäten, wie Diskussionsforen, Lancieren von Presseartikel, Imageanzeigen etc. bedienen, um die öffentliche Meinung für sich zu gewinnen. Ziel ist es nicht, die Gegner zu diffamieren.

Aufschwungsphase: Die zunehmende Diskussion um das Issue findet mit der breiten Öffentlichkeit statt. Durch die Berichterstattung der Medien wird das Issue nun in die Öffentlichkeit getragen und erhöht demzufolge den Problemlösungsdruck des Unternehmens. Die Anspruchsgruppen schalten sich ein und verlangen erste Lösungsvorschläge, wie politische Strategien oder Gesetzeserlassungen. Es bestehen somit potenzielle Ansprüche seitens der immer aktiveren Anspruchsgruppen. Die Organisationsinteressen können nur noch teilweise durchgesetzt werden, da eine immer größere Kompromissbereitschaft gefragt ist.

Reifephase: In dieser Phase werden Experten mit der Lösung des Problems beauftragt. Die Ansprüche konkretisieren sich immer mehr. Sobald sich jedoch offizielle Organe mit dem Issue in rechtförmiger Weise einschalten, bleiben dem Unternehmen nur noch folgende Optionen in Form von

- *politischen Verhandlungen*, in denen graduelle Zugeständnisse oder Reaktionen des Unternehmens bewirkt bzw. angedroht werden und
- *Lobbying* (Einwirkung auf Amtsträger oder Abgeordnete z. B. durch Bestechung oder Vorteilsversprechen).

Abschwungsphase: Die Lösung wird akut (aufgrund politischer Entscheidungen) umgesetzt und entsprechende Maßnahmen werden veranlasst, damit die gestellten Ansprüche weitestgehend befriedigt werden können. Es findet eine Anpassung des Unternehmens statt. Folglich sinkt auch wieder der Druck der Öffentlichkeit.

Um die Issues frühzeitig lenken und steuern zu können, bedarf es eines Issues Managements. Ingenhoff und Röttger (2006) definieren dieses wie folgt:

„Systematischer Kommunikationsprozess, der interne und externe Sachverhalte, die eine Begrenzung strategischer Handlungsspielräume erwarten lassen oder ein Reputationsrisiko darstellen, frühzeitig lokalisiert, analysiert, priorisiert und aktiv durch Maßnahmen zu beeinflussen versucht."

Der Issues-Management-Prozess (vgl. Ingenhoff und Röttger 2006, siehe Abb. 2.7) umfasst drei verschiedene Bereiche. Der erste Bereich (Variation) identifiziert

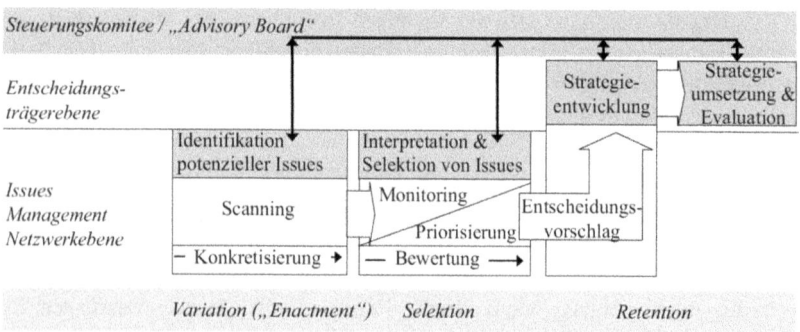

Abb. 2.7 Issue Management Prozess. Quelle: Ingenhoff und Röttger 2006

potenzielle Issues. Diese werden in einem nächsten Schritt (Selektion) interpretiert und selektiert, so dass die Issues bewertet und priorisiert werden. Die für ein oder mehrere Issues getätigte Entscheidung führt zu einer Strategieentwicklung, welchem Issue man sich wie widmen möchte (Retention).

2.2.7 Thema VII: Issue Management und Krisenkommunikation

In diesem thematischen Abschnitt geht es um das Zusammenspiel zwischen Issue Management und Krisenkommunikation (Abb. 2.8). Einschnitt und Beschreibungsmerkmal ist die Krise. Vor dem Kriseneintritt stehen als Präventionsmaßnahmen dem Unternehmen das Issue Management und das Risikomanagement zur Verfügung. Beim Issue Management geht es um das Entdecken potenzieller Problemfelder für das Unternehmen, um diese beim Risikomanagement zu bewerten. Dem Risikomanagement kommen auf der einen Seite das Vermeiden einer möglichen Krise als Aufgabe zu und auf der anderen Seite sollen Vorkehrungen getroffen werden, um im Krisenfall schnell zu reagieren. Das Krisenmanagement versucht, die eingetroffene Krise schnell zu bewältigen und zu lösen. Gleichzeitig findet das

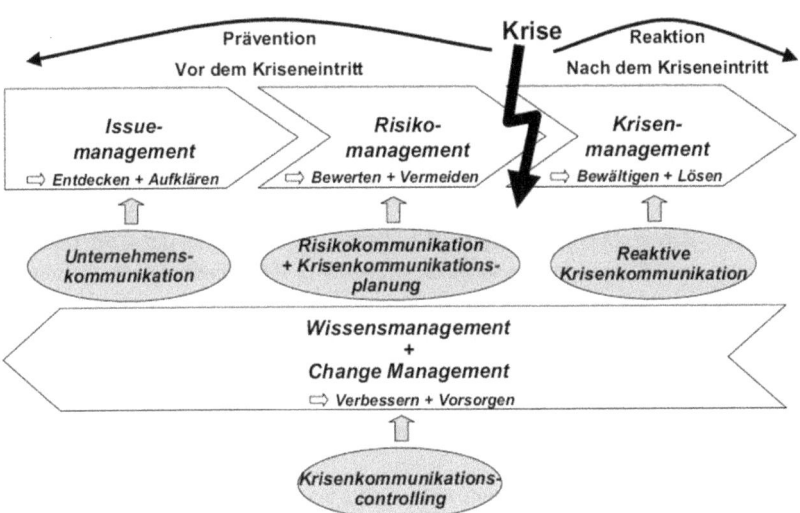

Abb. 2.8 Kommunikation im Krisenprozess. Quelle: Töpfer 2006

Krisenkommunikationscontrolling statt, welches die eigenen Maßnahmen beobachtet, speichert und bewertet (Wissensmanagement), um sie bei der nächsten Krise besser einsetzen zu können (Change Management).

2.2.8 Thema VIII: CSR

Das Unternehmen jpl 3 verschreibt sich bewusst dem Thema Corporate Social Responsibility. Dahlsrud (2008) kommt in seiner Untersuchung unterschiedlicher Definitionen von CSR zu dem Ergebnis, dass alle untersuchten Definitionen inhaltlich deckungsgleich sind und fünf Dimensionen umfassen: Stakeholderperspektive, sozial, ökonomisch, freiwillig und der Aspekt der Umwelt.

Diese fünf Dimensionen kommen in der vielzitierten Definition von Carroll und Shabana (2010) zum Ausdruck:

> „The social responsibility of business encompasses economic, legal, ethical, and philantrophic expectations that society has of organizations at a given point in time."

Die Gründe, warum Unternehmen CSR betreiben, sind vielfältig:
Neben der persönlichen Motivation des Unternehmers sind es vor allem folgende ökonomische Gründe:

- Kosten- und Risikoreduktion (Carroll und Shabana 2010): So können z. B. durch modernisierte Anlagen Strom und Wasser gespart werden.
- Steigerung der Arbeitgeberattraktivität (Schlegelmilch und Pollach 2005; Sen et al. 2006): Ein zunehmender Prozentsatz an Arbeitnehmern suchen sich ihren künftigen Arbeitgeber auch danach aus, ob und in welchem Ausmaß dieser CSR betreibt.
- Verbesserte Reputation (Carroll und Shabana 2010): Durch das CSR-Engagement eines Unternehmens kann die Reputation des Unternehmens gesteigert werden.
- Wettbewerbsvorteile durch CSR (Wang und Anderson 2011; Ingenhoff und Sommer 2011): Unternehmen, die CSR betreiben, können sich in den Augen der Konsumenten, denen dieser Aspekt wichtig ist, einen Wettbewerbsvorteil erschließen gegenüber Unternehmen, die keinerlei CSR-Engagement aufweisen.

Unternehmen, die CSR betreiben, stehen jedoch vor kommunikativen Herausforderungen. Erste Studien zeigen die Problematik der mangelnden Bekanntheit von CSR-Engagements (Dawkins 2005, Ingenhoff und Sommer 2011). Doch auch, wenn die Konsumenten auf das Engagement aufmerksam geworden sind, bestehen weitere Probleme. So reagieren die Stakeholder skeptisch auf das Engagement der Unternehmen (Du et al. 2010) nach dem Motto: Wer seine guten Absichten betont, dem glaubt man nicht.

Der heterogene Informationsbedarf der Stakeholder und die zunehmende gesellschaftliche Macht stellen die Unternehmen vor die Herausforderung, diesen adäquat zu begegnen und die Stakeholder im Rahmen eines Nachhaltigkeitskommunikations-Managements zu informieren. Dies erfordert einen kontinuierlichen Dialog, Partizipationsmöglichkeiten und effektive Kommunikationskonzepte. Im Mittelpunkt der Identifikation und Aushandlung der Ansprüche steht die Kommunikation mit den Stakeholdern.

2.2.9 Lehrpläne

Aus den vorgestellten Themengebieten lassen sich verschiedene Themen miteinander verbinden, so dass sich verschiedene Seminarplanungen je nach Zeitdauer und Schwerpunktgestaltung des Dozenten ergeben. In Tab. 2.2 und Tab. 2.3

Tab. 2.2 Seminarplan über acht Stunden

Themennummer	Dauer in Minuten	
	30	Organisatorisches/allgemeine Vorstellung
I	30	Shitstorm – Definition und Systematisierungsversuche
IV	30	Krisenkommunikation
V	60	Antwortstrategien
VIII	30	CSR
	20	Vorstellung der Case Study I
	60	Case Study I inkl. Zeigen des Videos und der Social-Media-Auftritte des Unternehmens jpl 3
	60	Gruppenbildung mit dem Ziel, Antwortstrategien für das Unternehmen jpl 3 zu entwickeln
	120	Vorstellung und Diskussion über mögliche Antwortstrategien
	440 (40 Minuten Puffer)	

Tab. 2.3 Seminarplan über mehr als 1000 Minuten

	Minuten		
	90	Kick-off, Ablauf der Veranstaltung, Erwartungen der Teilnehmer abfragen und in den Seminarplan einbeiten	
	90	Einführung in Case Studies (Was sind Case Studies? Welchen Nutzen haben sie?)	
I	90	Shitstorm – Definition und Systematisierungsversuche, Vorstellung verschiedener Shitstorms	
II, III	90	Social Media und Social-Media-Strategie	
IV	90	Krisenkommunikation	
V	90	Antwortstrategien	
VIII	90	CSR	
	90	Vorstellung der Case Study I; Case Study I inkl. Zeigen des Videos und der Social-Media-Auftritte des Unternehmens jpl 3	
	90	Bildung zweier Gruppen (Unternehmen und Konsumenten) mit dem Ziel, den Shitstorm von Konsumenten voranzutreiben und aus Unternehmenssicht, Antwortstrategien für das Unternehmen jpl 3 zu entwickeln.	
VI	90	Bildung zweier Gruppen (Unternehmen und Konsumenten) mit dem Ziel, den Shitstorm von Konsumenten voranzutreiben und aus Unternehmenssicht, Antwortstrategien für das Unternehmen jpl 3 zu entwickeln.	Issue Management / Prävention eines Shitstorms/ Issue Management und Krisenkommunikation
VII	90		
	90	Vorstellung und Diskussion über mögliche Antwortstrategien	
	90	Vorstellung der Case Study II, Abgleich mit den entwickelten Antwortstrategien	
	90	Diskussion über das mögliche Vorgehen von jpl 3 beim zweiten Shitstorm	
	90	Abschlussbesprechung	
	1260		

2.2 Lehrplan

beispielsweise Lehrpläne für ein achtstündiges und ein mehrwöchiges Seminar mit einem Stundenumfang von ca. 1000.

Beim Unternehmen jpl 3 handelt es sich um ein rein fiktionales Unternehmen. Jedoch wurde zur didaktischen Durchführung der Seminare eine Homepage entwickelt, ebenso wie ein Facebook – und Twitter-Auftritt.

So ist es möglich, gemeinsam mit den Teilnehmern, einen Shitstorm selbst zu initiieren und ihn aus Unternehmenssicht zu steuern/bändigen. Zu erreichen sind sie unter folgenden Adressen:

▶ Homepage: http://jpl3.jimdo.com/
Facebook: https://www.facebook.com/jpl3.shirtstories
Twitter: https://twitter.com/jpl3shirts

Anhang: Arbeitsblätter

Thema I und V Betrachten Sie die in Tab. 3.1 aufgelisteten anderen Shitstorms.

Aufgabe: Erstellen Sie aufgrund der bisherigen Beispiele die Merkmale eines Shitstorms.

Lösung:

- explosionsartige Entstehung und Verbreitung
- große Partizipation
- geschieht in der Öffentlichkeit
- tritt in Social Media auf und/oder wird durch Social Media verstärkt
- enthält subjektive Kritik
- enthält beleidigende Äußerungen
- hat eine affektive Komponente
- verlangt eine kommunikative Antwort
- kann eine krisenhafte Wirkung haben

Aufgabe: Betrachten Sie die jeweiligen Antworten der Unternehmen und erläutern Sie deren Strategien.

Lösung: Deutsche Bahn: Leugnen, Sündenbock
SinnLeffers: Entschuldigen
Vapiano: Angepasstes Informieren

Tab. 3.1 Shitstorms bei anderen Unternehmen

Nr.	Unternehmen (Monat/Jahr)	Inhalt/Auslöser des Shitstorms
1	Deutsche Bahn (Juli 2015)	Eine Kundin wollte eine erschöpfte Mitfahrerin ohne gültiges Ticket in ihr MVV-Abo einschließen. Der Kontrolleur akzeptierte dies nicht. Die Kundin schrieb dieses auf der Facebook-Seite des Unternehmens.
2	SinnLeffers (Juni 2015)	SinnLeffers verkauft Pullover der Boom Bap mit dem Aufdruck „Twinkle, Twinkle little whore, close your legs they´re not a door".
3	Vapiano (Februar 2014)	Ein Gast findet eine Raupe in seinem Gericht und postet ein Video bei Facebook.

Themen II und III

Aufgabe: Erstellen Sie eine Liste mit Ihnen bekannten Anwendungen/Homepages im Internet. Versuchen Sie, diese zu ordnen, indem Sie die jeweiligen Ziele, mit denen Personen diese nutzen, identifizieren.

Lösung: Social Media-Dreieck nach Schmidt (2011)

Aufgabe: Recherchieren Sie nach Social Media-Guidelines für Unternehmen im Internet. Schauen Sie sich diese an und vergleichen diese mit der Social Media-Strategie, die sie bereits durchgenommen haben. Sind diese Guidelines ausreichend oder fehlen Ihrer Meinung nach Aspekte?

Lösung: Social Media Guidelines sind oftmals sehr oberflächlich und geben keinerlei Hinweise für den Gebrauch von Social Media bei Krisen.

Themen IV, VI und VII

Aufgabe: Welche Variablen beeinflussen Ihrer Meinung nach das Verhalten von Unternehmen bei einem Krisenfall?

Lösung: Siah Ann Mei et al. (2010) unterscheiden in ihrer „new media crisis communication" zwischen prädisponierten und Situationsvariablen. Die Prädispositionsvariablen beeinflussen das Verhalten des Unternehmens beim Issue Management. Dazu zählen folgende Variablen:

Anhang: Arbeitsblätter

- Größe der Organisation
- Unternehmenskultur
- Darstellung des Unternehmens nach außen
- Zugang und Verhältnis zu den Stakeholdern
- Charakteristika der handelnden Akteure, wie z. B. der CEO
- Schaffen eines Bewusstseins, dass die Unternehmenskommunikation wichtig ist

Die Situationsvariablen hingegen beeinflussen die Reaktion auf die Krise. Zu diesen Variablen zählen:

- Dringlichkeit der Situation
- Charakteristika der involvierten Stakeholder
- Potenzielle Gefahren für das Unternehmen
- Potenzielle Kosten und Nutzen für das Unternehmen

Das Zusammenspiel dieser Variablen und das Verhalten von Unternehmen beim Issue Management und der Krisenkommunikation zeigt sich im prozesshaften new media crisis communication model (Siah Ann Mei 2010).

Literaturverzeichnis

Argenti P A, Druckenmiller B (2004) Reputation and the corporate brand. In: Corporate reputation review, 6 (4): 368–374

Carroll A B, Shabana K M (2010) The business case for corporate social responsibility: a review of concepts, research and practice. In: International Journal of Management Reviews, 12 (1) 85–105

Coombs T, Holladay S (2014) How publics react to crisis communication efforts. Journal of Communication Management, 18(1): 40–57

Coombs T, Holladay S (2015) CSR as crisis risk: expanding how we conceptualize the relationship, Corporate Communications: An International Journal, 20(2): S 144–162

Coombs W T (2010) Parameters for crisis communication. In: Coombs W T, Holladay S J (Hrsg) The Handbook of Crisis Communication, S 17–53

Coombs, W T (1998) An analytic framework for crisis situations: Better responses from a better understanding of the situation. Journal of Public Relations Research, 10(3): 177–191

Coombs, W T (2004) Impact of past crises on current crisis communication insights from Situational Crisis Communication Theory. Journal of business Communication, 41(3): 265–289

Coombs, W T (2006) The protective powers of crisis response strategies: Managing reputational assets during a crisis. Journal of Promotion Management, 12(3-4): 241–260

Coombs, W T (2007) Crisis management and communications. Institute for public relations, 4(5): 6

Coombs, W T (2007) Protecting Organization Reputations During a Crisis: The Development and Application of Situational Crisis Communication Theory. Corporate Reputation Review, 10(3): 163–176

Coombs, W T (2014) Ongoing crisis communication: Planning, managing, and responding. Thousand Oaks: Sage Publications

Coombs, W T (2014) State of Crisis Communication: Evidence and the Bleeding Edge. Research Journal of the Institute for Public Relations, 1(1)

Coombs W T, Holladay J (Hrsg) (2010) The Handbook of Crisis Communication. Hoboken: Wiley-Blackwell

Coombs W T, Holladay J (1996) Communication and attributions in a crisis: An experimental study in crisis communication. Journal of Public Relations Research, 8(4): 279–295

Dahlsrud A (2008) How corporate social responsibility is defined: an analysis of 37 definitions. Corporate social responsibility and environmental management, 15(1): 1

Dawkins J (2005) Corporate responsibility: The communication challenge. Journal of Communication Management, 9(2): 108–119

Dawson R (2009) Social Media Strategy Framework in German – Social Media strategische Rahmenrichtlinien – Trends in the Living Networks. http://rossdawsonblog.com/weblog/archives/2009/09/social_media_st_1.html (Zugegriffen: 08.11.2016)

Du S, Bhattacharya C B, Sen S (2010) Maximizing business returns to corporate social responsibility (CSR): The role of CSR communication. International Journal of Management Reviews, 12(1): 8–19

Himmelreich, S/Einwiller, S (2015) Wenn der „Shitstorm" überschwappt – Eine Analyse digitaler Spillover in der deutschen Print- und Onlineberichterstattung. In: Hoffjann, O, Pleil, T (Hrsg) Strategische Onlinekommunikation. Wiesbaden, S 183–205

Ingenhoff D, Röttger U (2006) Issues Management. In: Schmid, B, Lyczek, B (Hrsg) Unternehmenskommunikation, S 319–350. Wiesbaden: Gabler

Ingenhoff D, Sommer K (2011) Corporate social responsibility communication. Journal of Corporate Citizenship, 2011(42): 73–91

Kaiser F-J (1983) Grundlagen der Fallstudiendidaktik-Historische Entwicklung-Theoretische Grundlagen-Unterrichtliche Praxis. In: Die Fallstudie-Theorie und Praxis der Fallstudiendidaktik. Bad Heilbrunn, S 9–34

Kaplan A M, Haenlein M (2010) Users of the world, unite! The challenges and opportunities of Social Media. Business Horizons, 53(1): 59–68

Lobo S (2010) How to survive a shitstorm. http://saschalobo.com/2010/04/22/how-to-survive-a-shitstorm/ (Zugegriffen: 08.11.2016)

o. V. (2015) Medienwissenschaftler Pörksen kontert Nuhr-Kritik: "Wir müssen lernen, den Shitstorm zu lesen" http://meedia.de/2015/07/21/medienwissenschaftler-poerksen-kontert-nuhr-kritik-wir-muessen-lernen-den-shitstorm-zu-lesen/ (Zugegriffen: 08.11.2016)

Pfeffer J, Zorbach T, Carley K M (2014) Understanding online firestorms: Negative word-of-mouth dynamics in social media networks. Journal of Marketing Communications, 20(1-2): 117–128

Schaefer M (2010) An easy way to explain the social web. Really! – Schaefer Marketing Solutions: We Help Businesses {grow}. http://www.businessesgrow.com/2010/03/16/an-easy-way-to-explain-the-social-web-really/ (Zugegriffen: 08.11.2016)

Schlegelmilchsn B B, Pollach I (2005) The perils and opportunities of communicating corporate ethics. Journal of Marketing Management, 21(3-4): 267–290

Schmidt, J H (2011) Das neue Netz: Merkmale, Praktiken und Folgen des Web 2.0 [The new web: Characteristics, practices and consequences of the Web 2.0]

Sen S, Bhattacharya C B, Korschun D (2006) The role of corporate social responsibility in strengthening multiple stakeholder relationships: A field experiment. Journal of the Academy of Marketing science, 34(2): 158–166

Thießen A (2011) Organisationskommunikation in Krisen. Reputationsmanagement durch situative, integrierte und strategische Krisenkommunikation. Univ., Diss.-Fribourg, 1. Aufl. Wiesbaden

Töpfer A (2006) Krisenkommunikation. In: Schmid B, Lyczek B (Hrsg) Unternehmenskommunikation, S 351–398. Wiesbaden: Gabler

Wang A, Anderson R B (2011) A multi-staged model of consumer responses to CSR communications. Journal of Corporate Citizenship, 2011(41): 50–68

Weiterführende Literatur

Bekmeier-Feuerhahn S, Bögel P M (2015) CSR-Kommunikation: Gute Aussichten im Dialog?. In: Erkenntnis und Fortschritt: Beiträge aus Personalforschung und Managementpraxis. Festschrift für Albert Martin, S 86

Bryce K.R. (2014) The Role of Social Media in Crisis Management at Carnival Cruise Line. In: Journal of Business Case Studies (Online), 10(3): 231–238

Carroll C E (2015) The Handbook of Communication and Corporate Reputation. Hoboken: Wiley-Blackwell

Chan Y Y, Ngai E (2011) Conceptualising electronic word of mouth activity. In: Marketing Intelligence & Planning, 29(5): 488–516

Cheng S S (2013) Crisis Communication Failure: A Case Study of Typhoon Morakot. In: Asian Social Science, 9(3

Colleoni E (2013) CSR communication strategies for organizational legitimacy in social media. In: Corporate Communications: An International Journal, 18(2): 228–248

Conway T, Ward M, Lewis G, Bernhardt A (2007) Internet Crisis Potential: The Importance of a Strategic Approach to Marketing Communications. Journal of Marketing Communications, 13(3): 213–228

Einwiller S A, Steilen S (2015) Handling complaints on social network sites – An analysis of complaints and complaint responses on Facebook and Twitter pages of large US companies. Public Relations Review, 41(2): 195–204

Esch F-R, Tomczak T, Kernstock J, Langner T, Redler J (Hrsg) (2014) Corporate Brand Management. Wiesbaden

Gaßner, V (2014) CSR-Kommunikation: Chancen und Risiken eines offenen Dialogs mit Kunden und Kritikern im Social Web. In: Wagner R, Lahme G, Breitbarth T (Hrsg) CSR und Social Media. Berlin, Heidelberg, S 203–215

Geyer S, Krumay B (2015) Development of a Social Media Maturity Model — A Grounded Theory Approach. In: System Sciences (HICSS): 1859–1868

Goodman M B, Byrd S (2012) Hi fans! Tell us your story!. In: Corporate Communications: An International Journal, 17(3): 241–254

Hegner S M, Beldad A D, Kamphuis op Heghuis Sjarlot (2014) How company responses and trusting relationships protect brand equity in times of crises. Journal of Brand Management, 21(5): 429–445

Heinrich P (Hrsg) (2013) CSR und Kommunikation. Berlin, Heidelberg

Hennig-Thurau T, Gwinner K P, Walsh G, Gremler D D (2004) Electronic word-of-mouth via consumer-opinion platforms: What motivates consumers to articulate themselves on the Internet?. Journal of Interactive Marketing, 18(1): 38–52

Herrero A G, Pratt C B (1996) An integrated symmetrical model for crisis-communications management. Journal of Public Relations Research, 8(2): 79–105

Hoffjann O, Pleil T (Hrsg) (2015) Strategische Onlinekommunikation. Wiesbaden

Holladay S J (2009) Crisis Communication Strategies in the Media Coverage of Chemical Accidents. Journal of Public Relations Research, 21(2): 208–217

Holladay S J, Coombs W T (2013) Successful prevention may not be enough: A case study of how managing a threat triggers a threat. Public Relations Review, 39(5): 451–458

Huang Y-H (2008) Trust and Relational Commitment in Corporate Crises: The Effects of Crisis Communicative Strategy and Form of Crisis Response. Journal of Public Relations Research, 20(3): 297–327

Husain K, Abdullah A N, Ishak M, Kamarudin M F, Robani A, Mohin M, Hassan Syed Najmuddin Syed (2014) A Preliminary Study on Effects of Social Media in Crisis Communication from Public Relations Practitioners' Views. Procedia – Social and Behavioral Sciences, 155: 223–227

Ihlen Ø (2002) Defending the Mercedes A-class: Combining and changing crisis-response strategies. Journal of Public Relations Research, 14(3): 185–206

Kernstock J, Wenger-Schubiger N (2014) Public Relations im Dienste der Corporate Brand gestalten. In: Esch F-R, Tomczak T, Kernstock J, Langner T, Redler J (Hrsg) Corporate Brand Management. Wiesbaden, S 329–343

Kietzmann J, Canhoto A (2013) Bittersweet! Understanding and Managing Electronic Word of Mouth. Journal of Public Affairs, 13(2): 146–159

Liu B F, Austin L, Jin, Y (2011) How publics respond to crisis communication strategies: The interplay of information form and source. Public Relations Review, 37(4): 345–353

Liu B F, Jin, Y, Briones R, Kuch B (2012) Managing Turbulence in the Blogosphere: Evaluating the Blog-Mediated Crisis Communication Model with the American Red Cross. Journal of Public Relations Research, 24(4): 353–370

Lux W (2013) CSR-Kommunikation im Handel. In: Heinrich P (Hrsg) CSR und Kommunikation. Berlin, Heidelberg, S 133–145

Ly-Le T-M (2015) Danlait´s 2013 Social Media Crisis in Vietnam: A Case Study to Explore Online Crisis Scanning Criteria

Lyon L, Camero, G T (2004) A Relational Approach Examining the Interplay of Prior Reputation and Immediate Response to a Crisis. Journal of Public Relations Research

Manso M, Manso B (2012) The Role of Social Media in Crisis. Tekever Lisbon (Portugal)

Mavridis T (2011) Social Media Relations. Die neue Dimension der Nachhaltigkeitskommunikation. uwf UmweltWirtschaftsForum, 19(3-4): 245–248

McCorkindale T, Distaso M W, Carroll C E (2013) The Power of Social Media and Its Influence on Corporate Reputation. In: The Handbook of Communication and Corporate Reputation, S 497–512

Mehdizadeh S (2010) Self-Presentation 2.0: Narcissism and Self-Esteem on Facebook. In: Cyberpsychology, Behavior, and Social Networking, 13(4): 357–364

Merten K (2009) Zur Theorie des Gerüchts. Publizistik, 54(1): 15–42

Nauroth P, Gollwitzer M, Bender J, Rothmund T (2015) Social identity threat motivates science-discrediting online comments. PloS one, 1o(2): e0117476

Ott L, Theunissen P (2015) Reputations at risk: Engagement during social media crises. Public Relations Review, 41(1): 97–102

Weiterführende Literatur

Padgett D R G, Cheng S S, Parekh V (2013) The Quest for Transparency and Accountability: Communicating Responsibly to Stakeholders in Crises. Asian Social Science 9(9)

Pang A, Begam Binte Abul Hassan, Nasrath, Chee Yang Chong, Aaron (2014) Negotiating crisis in the social media environment. Corporate Communications: An International Journal, 19(1): 96–118

Röhner J, Schütz A (2012) Klassische Kommunikationstheorien und -modelle. In: Röhne, J, Schütz A (Hrsg) Psychologie der Kommunikation, Wiesbaden, S 15–33

Röhner J, Schütz A (Hrsg) (2012) Psychologie der Kommunikation. Wiesbaden

Romenti S, Murtarelli G, Valentini C (2014) Organisations' conversations in social media: applying dialogue strategies in times of crises. Corporate Communications: An International Journal, 19(1): 10–33

Schmid B, Lyczek B (Hrsg) (2006) Unternehmenskommunikation. Wiesbaden: Gabler

Schultz F, Utz S, Göritz A (2011) Is the medium the message? Perceptions of and reactions to crisis communication via twitter, blogs and traditional media. Public Relations Review, 37(1): 20–27

Schwarz A, Pforr F (2011) The crisis communication preparedness of nonprofit organizations: The case of German interest groups. Public Relations Review, 37(1): 68–70

Siah Ann Mei J, Bansal N, Pang A (2010) New media: a new medium in escalating crises?. Corporate Communications: An International Journal, 15(2): 143–155

Sisco H F (2012) Nonprofit in Crisis: An Examination of the Applicability of Situational Crisis Communication Theory. Journal of Public Relations Research, 24(1): 1–17

Sohn Y J, Lariscy, R (2012) Resource-Based Crisis Management: The Important Role of the CEO's Reputation. Journal of Public Relations Research, 24(4): 318–337

Sohn Y J, Lariscy R W (2014) Understanding reputational crisis: Definition, properties, and consequences. Journal of Public Relations Research, 26(1): 23–43

Steinke L (2014) Bedienungsanleitung für den Shitstorm. Wie gute Kommunikation die Wut der Masse bricht. Wiesbaden

Stephens K K, Malone P C (2009) If the Organizations Won't Give Us Information…: The Use of Multiple New Media for Crisis Technical Translation and Dialogue. Journal of Public Relations Research, 21(2): 229–239

Stich L, Golla G, Nanopoulos A (2014) Modelling the spread of negative word-of-mouth in online social networks. Journal of Decision Systems, 23(2): 203–221

Stoffels H, Bernskötter P (2012) Die Goliath-Falle. Die neuen Spielregeln für die Krisenkommunikation im Social Web, Wiesbaden

Thießen A (Hrsg) (2014) Handbuch Krisenmanagement. 2. Aufl. Wiesbaden

Utz S, Schultz F, Glocka S (2013) Crisis communication online: How medium, crisis type and emotions affected public reactions in the Fukushima Daiichi nuclear disaster. Public Relations Review, 39(1): 40–46

van der Meer TGLA, Verhoeven P (2013) Public framing organizational crisis situations: Social media versus news media. Public Relations Review, 39(3): 229–231

Veil S R, Buehner T, Palenchar M J (2011) A Work-In-Process Literature Review: Incorporating Social Media in Risk and Crisis Communication. Journal of Contingencies and Crisis Management, 19(2): 110–122

Wagner R, Lahme G, Breitbarth T (Hrsg) (2014) CSR und Social Media. Berlin, Heidelberg

Wetzer I M, Zeelenberg M, Pieters R (2007) "Never eat in that restaurant, I did!": Exploring why people engage in negative word-of-mouth communication. Psychology and Marketing, 24(8): 661–680

GPSR Compliance
The European Union's (EU) General Product Safety Regulation (GPSR) is a set of rules that requires consumer products to be safe and our obligations to ensure this.

If you have any concerns about our products, you can contact us on

ProductSafety@springernature.com

In case Publisher is established outside the EU, the EU authorized representative is:

Springer Nature Customer Service Center GmbH
Europaplatz 3
69115 Heidelberg, Germany

www.ingramcontent.com/pod-product-compliance
Ingram Content Group UK Ltd.
Pitfield, Milton Keynes, MK11 3LW, UK
UKHW021256180426
11947UKWH00011B/801

Praise for *Innovation in the Family Business*

"Is the concept of innovation in family business an oxymoron? Having coined the term 'interpreneurship' or 'intergenerational entrepreneurship' in 1989, my answer is a resounding no. Joe Schmieder proves the point. And his cases show you the way. Read this book!"
—Ernesto J. Poza, Clinical Professor, Global Entrepreneurship and Family Enterprise, Thunderbird School of Global Management, family business consultant, and author of *Family Business*

"In today's fast-paced world, innovation is not a luxury but a necessity. Schmieder has written an important and practical book that addresses how innovation can be created within the context and constraints of a family business. It's a must read for today's family business leaders."
—Joseph Horak, Ph.D., Director, Family Business Institute, Seidman College of Business, Grand Valley State University, Grand Rapids, Michigan

Innovation in the Family Business

A FAMILY BUSINESS PUBLICATION

Family Business Publications are the combined efforts of the Family Business Consulting Group and Palgrave Macmillan. These books provide useful information on a broad range of topics that concern the family business enterprise, including succession planning, communication, strategy and growth, family leadership, and more. The books are written by experts with combined experiences of over a century in the field of family enterprise and who have consulted with thousands of enterprising families the world over, giving the reader practical, effective, and time-tested insights to everyone involved in a family business.

The Family Business Consulting Group, Inc., founded in 1994, is the leading business consultancy exclusively devoted to helping family enterprises prosper across generations.

FAMILY BUSINESS LEADERSHIP SERIES

This series of books is comprised of concise guides and thoughtful compendiums to the most pressing issues that anyone involved in a family firm may face. Each volume covers a different topic area and provides the answers to some of the most common and challenging questions.

Titles include:

Developing Family Business Policies: Your Guide to the Future
Effective Leadership in the Family Business
Family Business Compensation
Family Business Governance: Maximizing Family and Business Potential
Family Business Ownership: How to Be an Effective Shareholder
Family Business Succession: The Final Test of Greatness
Family Business Values: How to Assure a Legacy of Continuity and Success
The Family Constitution: Agreements to Secure and Perpetuate Your Family and Your Business
Family Education for Business-Owning Families: Strengthening Bonds by Learning Together
Family Meetings: How to Build a Stronger Family and a Stronger Business
Financing Transitions: Managing Capital and Liquidity in the Family Business
From Siblings to Cousins: Prospering in the Third Generation and Beyond
How Families Work Together
How to Choose and Use Advisors: Getting the Best Professional Family Business Advice
Working for a Family Business: A Non-Family Employee's Guide to Success
Letting Go: Preparing Yourself to Relinquish Control of the Family Business
Make Change Your Family Business Tradition
More than Family: Non-Family Executives in the Family Business
Nurturing the Talent to Nurture the Legacy: Career Development in the Family Business
Preparing Successors for Leadership: Another Kind of Hero
Preparing Your Family Business for Strategic Change
Siblings and the Family Business: Making It Work for Business, the Family, and the Future
Managing Conflict in the Family Business: Understanding Challenges at the Intersection of Family and Business
Innovation in the Family Business: Succeeding Through Generations

All of the books were written by members of the Family Business Consulting Group and are based on both our experiences with thousands of client families as well as our empirical research at leading research universities the world over.

Innovation in the Family Business

Succeeding Through Generations

Joe Schmieder

palgrave
macmillan

INNOVATION IN THE FAMILY BUSINESS
Copyright © Family Business Consulting Group, 2014.
All rights reserved.

First published in 2014 by
PALGRAVE MACMILLAN®
in the United States—a division of St. Martin's Press LLC,
175 Fifth Avenue, New York, NY 10010.

Where this book is distributed in the UK, Europe and the rest of the world, this is by Palgrave Macmillan, a division of Macmillan Publishers Limited, registered in England, company number 785998, of Houndmills, Basingstoke, Hampshire RG21 6XS.

Palgrave Macmillan is the global academic imprint of the above companies and has companies and representatives throughout the world.

Palgrave® and Macmillan® are registered trademarks in the United States, the United Kingdom, Europe and other countries.

ISBN 978-1-137-38623-6   ISBN 978-1-137-38624-3 (eBook)
DOI 10.1057/9781137386243

Library of Congress Cataloging-in-Publication Data

Schmieder, Joe.
    Innovation in the family business : succeeding through generations / Joe Schmieder.
        pages cm.—(A family business publication)

    1. Family-owned business enterprises. 2. Small business—Management. 3. Management—Technological innovations. I. Title.
HD62.25.S36 2014
658.4'06—dc23   2014024360

A catalogue record of the book is available from the British Library.

Design by Newgen Knowledge Works (P) Ltd., Chennai, India.

First edition: December 2014

10 9 8 7 6 5 4 3 2 1

To Val, Maria, and Adam
For providing me the support and inspiration to spend
a lifetime working with family businesses

Contents

LIST OF FIGURES xi

SPECIAL RECOGNITION xiii

ACKNOWLEDGMENTS xv

INTRODUCTION: CREATING THE FUTURE—
LEADING THROUGH INNOVATION. xvii

1: The Family Business Difference: Capitalizing on
Family Innovation 1

2: Structured Chaos: Creating a Culture of
Innovation 15

3: New Products and Services: Driving Value
with Innovative Offerings 33

4: Money and Metrics: Funding and Measuring
Innovation 51

5: The Next Generation: Reinnovating the Family
Business 61

6: Leadership and Ownership Transitions:
Ensuring Succession Supports Innovation 73

7: Governance: Overseeing Key Relationships to
Support Innovation 89

8: Moving Innovation Forward: Concluding
Thoughts 107

NOTES 113

ABOUT THE AUTHOR 117

INDEX 119

Figures

3.1 Focus of family business innovation resources 35

3.2 Stage-Gate New Product Process 42

3.3 WinOvations New Product Development Process . . . 43

3.4 A-to-F Method for Innovation Success 46

3.5 MVA Innovation Framework diagram 48

7.1 The 3-Circle model: the board of directors, the family council, and the executive team 92

7.2 Simplified Governance Structure 93

7.3 Evolution of Family Business Board Forms 94

7.4 The Family Business Territories 100

Special Recognition

I wish to recognize the important contributions of the University of Notre Dame's Mendoza College of Business. Mendoza is a recognized source of original thought on the management of family enterprise and an inspiring force behind the creation of this book. In particular, I acknowledge Dean Roger Huang and his predecessor, Dean Carolyn Woo, whose support and foresight were instrumental in the completion of this book.

Acknowledgments

Many family business members, colleagues, scholars, advisors, and people in the publishing domain have helped bring this book to life.

I am especially grateful to those enterprising families who were willing to contribute their stories, for it is through shared family business experiences that other families gain the most applicable knowledge and motivation to incorporate innovation into their own firms.

I greatly appreciate the ongoing insights of my colleagues at the Family Business Consulting Group (FBCG). John L. Ward—cofounder of FBCG and noted family business advisor, professor, and author—ignited the challenge to dive deeper into the topic of innovation and provided keen guidance throughout the writing process. Chris Eckrich, my teaching partner at the University of Notre Dame and fellow principal at FBCG, made sure innovation was included as a topic in the classroom, helping to refine many concepts in this book.

Laurie Harting, Executive Editor at Palgrave Macmillan, continuously coached me in developing a logical structure with meaningful content for family business members. Sachin Waikar reviewed every story and every word, enhancing the copy to maximize its flow, relevance, and impact. Julie Lucas and Heather Noordyke worked tirelessly to pull together all the details of the nearly 50 stories cited in the book. Notre Dame intern Hannah Meckstroth and independent researcher Michelle Hoxum compiled important data that helped shed light on key elements of family business innovation.

At home in West Michigan, a highly fertile ground for family businesses, I am thankful for the many family business leaders who have demonstrated how innovation can make a difference for their family firms. Most notably, Tim Schad, Chairman of fourth-generation Nucraft Furniture Company, consistently offered ideas and encouragement.

Finally, I want to thank my family—Val, Maria and Adam—not only for encouraging me to write this book but for understanding the large investment of time and energy it required.

Thank you all for your support and guidance.

Introduction: Creating the Future—Leading Through Innovation

As a young girl, Mary had always loved spending time in the Heritage Room at Markers Enterprise in Danbury, Connecticut. Lined with long-discontinued artifact textile products and faded company picnic photos from years gone by, the room created an aura of nostalgia and pride. For over 130 years, the Marker family had grown a successful business, starting with durable horsehide tanning processes and evolving into modern shoes and a variety of other clothing offerings.

Now in her 40s, Mary still enjoyed visiting the small-scale family business museum regularly. She marveled at the determination and ingenuity previous generations had demonstrated in continuously developing innovative products and practices to address shifts in both the business and the family arenas. In thinking about the family's rich heritage, Mary was doing more than admiring her ancestors' efforts: she was seeking inspiration. She, two siblings, and two cousins were fourth-generation family members who worked in the enterprise. Although the family and its business challenges had grown dramatically over the decades, Mary's generation faced the same question its predecessors had: how could they continue the innovation legacy, creating new offerings and business approaches, so that the family and its business would continue to prosper for future generations?

This book is meant to help people like Mary and others interested in innovation in family business. *My purpose in writing it is to inspire enterprising families to focus more energy and resources on innovation throughout their family businesses, and to provide them some ideas for creative directions to pursue on multiple dimensions.*

THE IMPORTANCE OF INNOVATIVENESS

The premise of this book is that *innovativeness* can be considered one of four factors associated with multigeneration family business prosperity and longevity. The three factors that have already emerged from a review of the FBCG's (The Family Business Consulting Group) multigeneration clients across sectors are

- strategic planning,
- independent board members, and
- family meetings.

Innovation is important to any kind of business. In fact, Robert G. Cooper, author of numerous publications on new product and service development, suggests, "The single strongest predictor of business value is the degree of innovativeness of the company."[1] Many of the most highly esteemed sources for business research and thinking—including Harvard Business School, *Forbes Magazine*, MIT Sloan, and McKinsey—have supported this assertion for a wide range of firms, including publicly owned ones. According to a recent Boston Consulting Group article, "For most companies, innovation is the key to driving growth, value for shareholders, and competitive advantage in today's global economy."[2]

We need look no further than well-known technology companies like Apple and Google for evidence of the value of *product* and *marketing* innovations; ongoing innovativeness has boosted their revenues, profits, and stock prices dramatically. Does the same correlation between *innovation and value* hold for family firms? Although much more difficult to quantify because the data are confidential (most family firms are privately held), there is growing evidence that family firms that demonstrate adaptability, such as a propensity for creative change and adjustment to marketplace trends and customer needs, do in fact increase their value and longevity.

Let's take a step back and define the term "innovation," as it has been overused in recent years and has many interpretations within the media and among the general public. In the most basic terms, innovation is *change*. For our purposes, in the context of family business, we will consider it *creative change that produces meaningful results*. This implies that change merely for the sake of change is not innovative. Change that produces a meaningful, or ultimately commercially successful, outcome is innovative.

Beyond that basic definition, innovation comes in multiple forms. Most visibly, innovation appears in the form of new products, from the oft-cited caveman's stone wheel to the latest digital phone. Game-changing products emerge from fresh thinking and actions that lead to applicable, relevant results. But not all products are as profound in their impact as the first wheel or the iPhone. Most creative changes are far less visible and reflect an evolutionary process, such as using wood to make a lighter and faster wheel than one made of stone.

Importantly, many innovations are not even related to product or service offerings. Less visible, but high-impact, innovations come in the form of business models, processes, and structures. In many cases, these often-unheralded innovations produce key results for the family business. They include outcomes like creative estate planning for transfer of ownership, unique ways to prepare the next generation for leadership, and clever organization structures that blend family and nonfamily leaders. Long-enduring family businesses have found ways to incorporate a range of innovations that have led to business and family success.

WHY IT MATTERS

Innovation in family enterprise matters because family businesses drive the majority of global commerce: 70 percent to 90 percent of the world's gross domestic product, according to the Family Firm Institute.[3] Long recognized as the dominant business system worldwide, family business has sparked ongoing research to understand its overwhelming long-term success. For 20 years, the FBCG has had the privilege to work with over 2,000 enterprising family businesses of all ages and sizes to help them grow and prosper. Over the years, FBCG has developed working definitions of a family business. The definition used in this book is *a business, family office, or family foundation where the ownership is controlled by a family or a small group of families with some level of active leadership or participation in the business.* Whether it is a small to mid-sized business such as a local automotive dealership that bears the family name, or a huge multinational corporation such as Cargill, the largest privately owned family business in the United States, the family businesses used in this book meet this definition.

This book builds upon the growing body of existing innovation-related research and combines these findings with real-life family company experiences to derive a set of elements and practices that can inspire and inform innovation throughout a family business. The book shares a broad range of tools and pathways that family businesses across sectors use to stimulate, execute, measure, and reward change within their family business, across dimensions. The 50-plus family stories cited in this book are (1) real and approved for use by the family business described, (2) part of the public domain, or (3) fictionalized portraits of real family businesses with identifying factors (names, locations, dates) changed to protect enterprise members and to further enhance the learning points. In short, many of the examples presented here are derived from the FBCG's and my own work with enterprising families. Great care has been taken to protect all confidential information. In this way we can help other family businesses take an innovative approach without compromising their peers who have inspired the book's content. Boosting any family enterprise's level of innovation will ensure it maintains profitability and contributes to the global economy for decades to come.

WHAT'S IN THIS BOOK

There is an assortment of excellent literature on innovation in business. Likewise, there are many excellent publications on family business. Yet few authors have attempted to address specifically the *intersection of innovation and family business*. The efforts to focus on this area so far have highlighted the need for

- a culture of innovation,
- a process for innovation,
- integration of innovation throughout the family business,

- inclusion of family members in innovation, and
- clear ways to fund and measure innovation.

These findings helped shape this book's content and structure. The chapters are laid out as follows:

1. *The Family Difference—Capitalizing on Family Innovation.* This chapter explores the drivers that make family enterprises different from other businesses, especially in the context of innovation; differentiating features include family business's longer-term time horizons and focus on incremental versus radical change.
2. *Structured Chaos—Creating a Culture of Innovation.* This chapter discusses the rationale for creating a culture that supports innovation in family business, along with ideas for how to do so.
3. *Core Offerings—Driving Value with Products and Service Innovations.* This chapter considers how families can incorporate a process for developing original products and services, the largest domain of innovation in family enterprise.
4. *Money and Metrics—Funding and Measuring Innovation.* This chapter highlights approaches to funding innovation and measuring its outcomes on multiple dimensions.
5. *The Next Generation—Reinnovating the Family Business.* This chapter examines how to promote an innovative approach among the rising generation of family business leaders.
6. *Leadership and Ownership Transitions—Ensuring Succession Supports Innovation.* This chapter explores how succession among leaders and owners can both support change and be innovative in itself.
7. *Governance—Overseeing Key Relationships to Support Innovation.* This chapter discusses the mutually reinforcing role of governance bodies, including the board of directors and family council, in supporting innovation, along with considering the unique roles of individuals throughout multiple "territories" of the enterprise.
8. *Moving Innovation Forward—Concluding Thoughts.* As a wrap-up, this chapter integrates lessons from the previous chapters and provides parting advice for families looking to step-up their level of innovation.

The topics, examples, and suggestions offered throughout the book are expected to generate meaningful conversations and further research on innovation in family business. For those family businesses just embarking on their own unique innovation journey, the book is designed to be read in sequence. For those family businesses further along the innovation path, it will likely be of greater value to pick chapters or sections of chapters to read, as suited to the business's needs.

Ultimately, I hope the content inspires enterprising families, including those like Mary's at Marker, to take a more intentional, thoughtful, and ultimately successful approach to innovation, which will help promote their long-term continuity.

Chapter 1

The Family Business Difference: Capitalizing on Family Innovation

"How did Grandpa and Great Aunt Millie start the family business?"

Ten-year-old Billy Douglas asked his father that as they sat with other relatives around a campfire. It was a cool September Sunday evening, and the extended family had gathered for a reunion at their historic Iowa homestead. In recent years, Billy had heard bits and pieces of how the family's agricultural products business began. It was a rich opportunity for his father, William, to share the full story of its origin, a story that highlighted the many benefits of family businesses.

Billy's grandfather, Ed Douglas, had always been well liked in his community, and had a clear interest in entrepreneurship. In the late 1940s, he owned a farm outside Des Moines, Iowa. He decided to branch out into selling fertilizer off the back of his Ford pickup truck, aided by his sister, Millie. Observing how much they and their farmer customers—and they themselves—struggled to improve their yields of corn and other crops, the siblings were interested in new soil-preparation approaches. Most of the large agricultural suppliers that served the area were less willing to experiment with fertilizers and other products.

"Why not develop our own fertilizer?" Ed said to Millie one spring day. They had heard about the possibility of using anhydrous ammonia, an inorganic fertilizer (82% nitrogen), to help replace the essential nutrients needed for healthy crops. Millie was excited about the prospect, but they had few tangible assets to dedicate to the venture: an aging John Deere tractor, a modified Hobart mixer in which to try new fertilizer formulas, a dozen-odd barrels to hold materials, and a small old barn for storage. At the same time, the Douglas siblings had several *intangible* assets: close relationships with local farmers (to help them understand market needs), deep experience with conditions affecting crop yield (based largely on their own farming), courage to try new approaches to increase yields, and patience to wait for the growing cycle in order to prove the effectiveness (or lack thereof) of their fertilizers.

Based on these assets—and their commitment to reduce their dependence on unpredictable crop yields—Ed and Millie decided to make and sell their own fertilizer. However, because they each had a growing family (eight children altogether, including Will, Billy's father), they were unwilling to bet the farm, literally, on the new venture. They decided to launch the business on top of their day-to-day farming duties, with Millie mixing the fertilizer, and Ed selling and delivering it.

And so Duration Ag Products was born.

Long-standing family values of hard work, creative problem solving, and experimentation were evident in Ed and Millie's approach from the start. They worked tirelessly on new products, keeping careful track of what worked and what did not work, always soliciting feedback from customers. After several years of formulating, testing, and reformulating mixtures, they found a winning combination that consistently improved crop output. So in 1953, Millie and Ed transitioned their farm duties to several siblings, cousins, and hired hands and focused their full-time efforts on the business. They were eventually joined by several of their children, including William.

Over the next 60 years, Duration Ag grew into a business with over $100 million in sales and over 300 employees, serving domestic and international customers in 15 countries. The company's offerings expanded dramatically, from one chemical fertilizer to multiple fertilizer types (hot-mix, cold-mix, suspension, and dry), limestone, agricultural chemicals, soil-testing products, micronutrients, feed, seed, and technical support. Of course, the two generations had to overcome many challenges to succeed, including the need to rebuild after a large fire in 1967 and the inability to collect almost a third of their receivables because of the impact of interest rate spikes on customers in the 1980s.

Several factors went into Duration Ag's ongoing success. One was the owners' emphasis on operating with minimal debt; another was its long-term view. The family also relied on strong, long-standing ties with its bankers, attorneys, and accountants, several of whom also came from family businesses. For example, their estate-planning attorney and accountant had helped them keep all shares within the family to the present day, including the use of a gifting process to transfer ownership between the first and second generations (and soon to the third, Billy's cohort). The business had also hired experienced executives, including an agronomist with an advanced degree as head of research and development (R&D). This professional helped them develop cutting-edge fertilizer formulations, including foliar nutrients and crop protection products with additional environmental benefits.

Grateful to the community that had supported their business and eager to give back, the family donated a community foundation center—named the Douglas Foundation Center—to their hometown. They also continued a long-standing tradition of providing assistance in the form of scholarships and grants to the communities, farms, and families with which they did business.

Now firmly established as a mid-sized player in a mature market, Duration Ag faced new pressures as it prepared to transition ownership to the next generation. Among the challenges were increasingly strict and complex environmental regulations, mounting foreign competition, higher ingredient pricing from large chemical companies, and determination of the best business/governance roles for the 12 third-generation cousins (including Billy) who may have wished to join the business.

Resolving these issues would require new solutions built on the same kind of innovation that had taken Duration Ag from a few barrels of fertilizer in a barn to a $100 million multigeneration business.

* * *

THE FAMILY BUSINESS DIFFERENCES

Duration Ag exemplifies how most family enterprises represent a living business organism that is quite distinct from nonfamily firms. Specifically, the overlap of family and business creates a tight connection unique to family firms. In most cases, family members are owners *and* operating leaders of the business until it grows to a size and complexity best served by a blend of family ownership and professional executive leadership. Thus the business's success correlates directly to the family's well-being, and the family's economic well-being correlates directly to the business's success. On one hand, that can mean that family enterprises "are further complicated by the close proximity of these dual relationships because family members simultaneously participate in both business and family relationships, in their personal and professional lives."[1] On the other, it can mean that family businesses have unique strengths built on the overlap of family and business, in part because the family running the business has more at stake—including reputation, survival, and security—than the managers and employees of nonfamily firms do.

Innovation is one such strength at the family business intersection. Innovation in a family business, like most other features, is different from that in nonfamily firms. A key difference is that innovation in family firms is driven and enhanced by several distinct factors that can ultimately yield greater business performance and family harmony. The drivers include

- personal attachments,
- incremental versus radical innovation ("Everything in moderation"),
- a longer-term horizon,
- shared values over shared profits (definition of success),
- low leverage (independence from capital markets),
- experimental tolerance, and
- family leadership (decision-making).

The remainder of this chapter describes each of these innovation drivers in detail, with examples from innovative family businesses.

PERSONAL ATTACHMENTS

In a family enterprise, business performance and risk are deeply personal. Launching and growing Duration Ag directly impacted the family's financial status, reputation, employment opportunities, and ultimately their legacy. It was a positive impact in the Douglas family's case. On the flip side, the consequences can be quite negative, as many families have discovered firsthand, such as when a family business decimates a family's life savings and creates dysfunctional behavior, including interpersonal conflict. But personal attachments, as defined here, also include relationships the family maintains within and outside their family group and enterprise. Each of these elements can distinguish a family business from a nonfamily firm and help drive innovation in the former.

Consider the types of personal attachments illustrated in the Duration Ag story. First, Ed and his sister, Millie, had a strong, trust-based *family bond* that allowed them to consider establishing a business together in the first place and made them more open to the others' ideas and perspectives, resulting in more diverse strategies and tactics. Their mutual trust also helped them separate responsibilities, like Millie's early focus on product development and Ed's on sales/delivery, and innovate together, encouraging each other to try and try again through countless failed products. Family bonds also enabled the siblings to borrow money from relatives who believed in their idea and potential. Those early funds—which would have been hard to secure from a bank or other nonfamily funding sources—helped support early innovation, which was crucial for the business. In general, family bonds may enable family business leaders to secure capital for creative developments, including those which stem from less conventional ideas.

Second, Ed and Millie maintained deep *customer relationships* built largely on their standing in the community, first as individuals and then as a family enterprise. These often long-standing and deep personal attachments allowed Ed and Millie to get to know local farmers' needs based on "insider knowledge" secured through confidential or less accessible communication channels, and to develop new offerings with these in mind. For example, when they heard through close customers that farmers wanted better access to fertilizer throughout the day, they installed a self-service facility with around-the-clock access, pleasing customers and boosting revenues. Moreover, many of their early customers were families whom they had known for a long time, families who trusted them enough to allow testing of their early prototypes on small portions of their crops. These customer families would be more reticent to provide a faceless corporation the same privilege. Families help families.

That holds true for *interfamily business relationships*, as well. There is an informal but frequently vocalized code among family businesses of cooperating with one another across a range of activities. For example, in the United States alone there are approximately 50 active family business centers housed mostly at universities (such as Northwestern University's Center for Family Enterprises at the Kellogg School of Management) that bring family businesses together to share insights and best practices. Many of these shared ideas have to do with innovation, whether related to developing new products and processes or transferring ownership to the next generation.

Finally, the Duration Ag example includes evidence of *connections to external partners*, including financial and legal advisors, like the accountant and attorney who helped the family maintain and transfer ownership. Such long-term partners aid the family business in innovating and performing on multiple levels as they steward the enterprise for the sake of shareholders, future generations, and the broader community.

Not surprisingly, strong personal attachments are driven largely by the founders and the present leaders of the family business, who can help establish a culture that values personal ties. Even billion-dollar family enterprises continue to be well served by family leaders who stay personally involved, providing inspiring connections to the family and promoting "ambassador" relationships with employees, key customers, vendors, and community leaders. As the Amway Corporation grew from a garage-based operation into a multibillion-dollar company, it became even more important that the two family founders—Rich DeVos and Jay Van Andel—were out front kicking off business conventions, talking about new ideas, writing compelling newsletter articles, and meeting and greeting the prospective "independent business owners" who formed the corporation's marketing backbone. This personal touch not only provides deep motivation for nonfamily members to join the business family, but also helps promote firm-wide change and MODERNIZATION. People are always excited to work with a firm dedicated to changing with the times, and are willing to commit themselves to driving innovation for such businesses.

INCREMENTAL VERSUS RADICAL INNOVATION ("EVERYTHING IN MODERATION")

Groundbreaking new products—like the iPhone or Viagra—rarely emerge from family businesses. Family-run enterprises tend to prefer smaller-scale, incremental innovation over radical changes, in contrast to the publicly held Apples and Pfizers of the world, which have deep pockets for R&D funding. For most family enterprises, growing by incremental steps is preferable to advancing by giant leaps. This "incrementalist" approach dominates partly because family businesses are averse to assuming large risks and taking on large debt. Not surprisingly, then, family businesses tend to be quick followers or quick improvers, rather than original innovators. But we can argue that incrementalism represents a form of innovation, as it focuses on steady improvement of offerings or ways of doing business through meaningful change, in line with the definition of "innovation" provided in the Introduction.

Research suggests that successful, long-lasting family firms *exercise moderation* with regard to most key dimensions: planning, leverage, and innovation, among others. A 2013 study highlighted how family businesses tend to take an incremental approach to new product development, as part of a broader objective of careful resource management.[2] The moderation approach is related to the desire to maintain sufficient resources, financial and otherwise, for family shareholders. Thus, while venture capital firms talk about burn rate, or the amount of cash a start-up venture plows through in early stages, and how quickly a given innovation can be brought to market and scaled, family businesses tend to talk about less exciting things, like self-funded developments or modifications to existing products. That prompts some to believe that observing family firms innovate is like watching paint dry. In reality, however, steady progress is the key to success and continuity for many family businesses and nonfamily firms. The paint may take time to dry, but it sets very well, with deeper, longer-lasting color. Or, to use another analogy, many family businesses are like baseball players who make long, successful careers hitting singles and doubles, unlike their slugger peers who blast homeruns but strike out more often and tend to have shorter stints as professional ballplayers, on average.

The moderation approach to innovation has served most family businesses well: they evolve at a pace that fits them, based on collaborative thinking among family leaders and nonfamily executives who understand and adhere to the family's guiding principles. At the same time, the incrementalist approach may not always be ideal, especially in fast-shifting markets. Family businesses that fail to adapt quickly enough to the changing landscape will struggle to perform. The print media industry, for example, has been a high-profile sector populated by many family-owned firms (such as newspapers). In the new millennium, this market has undergone rapid transformation, mainly because of the rising popularity of nontraditional content-delivery channels, especially digital ones. Some family firms have adapted very well to the Digital Age, innovating digitally based strategies and offerings. Others have not adapted nearly as well, and are suffering greatly for it.

The highest-performing family businesses are those that have learned to be just innovative enough, like Goldilocks searching for the "just right" bowl of porridge in the bears' house. These businesses match their innovation speed to the requirements of their industry and the pace of their competition, moving more deliberately than many nonfamily peers, in part because they don't face the same kind of pressure for short-term results. The Douglas family built upon their first chemical fertilizer slowly, using a series of modifications and processes that helped them introduce cold-mix and hot-mix fertilizers, other specialty formulations, and soil-testing products. None of these new offerings was a major breakthrough product, but collectively they represented more of what their farming customers needed and wanted as times changed. For many family businesses, when it comes to innovation, slow is "fast," or is at least the right speed.

The Hendrick family behind Worden Company, a manufacturer of library furniture, offers a similar example, but one involving a different kind of innovation. As the family watched the library market shift from physical books and other reading material to digitally based information (such as e-books), they knew it was time to innovate. So the younger generation used its furniture knowledge to create a dynamic new offshoot company and product line named Sparkeology: furniture fitting the culture and needs of fast-growing tech companies, including acrylic-based pieces designed for open spaces. Again, while this wasn't necessarily a groundbreaking move, it was just enough innovation to help the enterprise adapt to changing times without overhauling its core values or offerings.

LONGER-TERM HORIZON

It is well known that family firms take a much longer view of the business and their return on investments than nonfamily businesses do. The greater time frame helps family businesses innovate in a slow and steady way, as discussed earlier. The longer-term horizon also endows family businesses with another trait crucial for successful innovation: patience. Whereas a publicly traded company has limited tolerance for missed deadlines—based largely on shareholder and analyst expectations—family firms enjoy the "luxury" of tolerance, with an inherent recognition that change takes time. While this patience is mostly a good thing, as discussed for our purposes, it can also be a disadvantage, as the overly tolerant family firm may delay necessary innovation excessively, take too long with development, or fail to innovate at all, resulting in lost value on all dimensions.

The good news is that the longer-term horizon embraced by family firms helps them overcome a major obstacle for innovation in *any* kind of business: development time. Most changes that result in commercial success, whether related to new products or processes, simply take longer than expected. Family businesses are much more likely than nonfamily firms to stick with a slow-moving but on-target innovation process, seeing it through more fully. Consider an example from the Douglas family of Duration Ag. While expanding their offerings to soil-testing materials, they spent *eight years* developing a set of products that delivered superior value over the competition's. They could have entered the market much more quickly with "me-too" products, but they knew that was a low-value strategy. The time they took paid off as they quickly won a growing share of the market with their CREATIVE products. When it comes to innovation, patience and the long view are truly virtues and drivers of meaningful change.

SHARED VALUES OVER SHARED PROFITS (DEFINITION OF SUCCESS)

For over 17 generations, the Mogi family has made sauce. Not just any sauce, but Kikkoman Soy Sauce, one of the best-known brands in the category. Part of the Japanese family's success and their company's longevity has been the family constitution they created in the late 1800s, including 16 guiding principles, or values. Principle Number 15 speaks to the trait of humility: "never think highly of yourself."[3] Such shared values are at the heart of many successful family enterprises, and they support strengths in innovation.

The importance of values in family business is well documented. John L. Ward, one of the founders of the Family Business Consulting Group (FBCG), says, "Values pervade every aspect of family business. Values are the independent variable shaping every dimension of family business management."[4] Truly enterprising families use their values to help guide key decisions regarding strategy, structure, diversification, culture, employee recruitment, governance, succession, and, of course, innovation. They consistently prioritize adherence to values over narrow focus on profits, recognizing that values are more likely to keep the family together and prosperous over generations.

At Michigan-based Byrne Electrical Specialists, designers and producers of electrical outlets used in furniture, airport counters, and other sites, the firm's values are clear from its vision: "to perpetuate the family business by staying ahead of the competition through innovation, effective problem solving, and rapid execution." Innovation is not only part of the business's vision but also one of its Key Strategic Focus Areas, described as the need to "pioneer new opportunities, create solutions." Byrne family executives create annual initiatives and objectives for each focus area, and one year the objective under innovation was to "Strive for market leadership in design, speed and risk management." This objective was supported by elements that included an enhanced product-development process to boost cross-functional visibility, increased investment in design training, and the implementation of design- and product-development-related feedback loops. Byrne's double-digit growth, three times greater than the rate of the industry, speaks to its ability to implement its explicit value of innovation.

In general, the strong values and vision of family firms can provide a foundation of security and stability that welcomes change and, more specifically, innovation.

LOW LEVERAGE (INDEPENDENCE FROM CAPITAL MARKETS)

Long-lasting family enterprises demonstrate a remarkably low level of debt in operating and growing the business. Once a family business navigates through its start-up phase, it is well served by taking great care handling capital, especially by avoiding heavy leverage (debt). Most successful family firms plow funds generated from the business back into the business, opting to build the enterprise over providing excessive distributions. And great family enterprises are patient with their capital, willing to innovate deliberately and wait patiently for returns. Again, some families can take this too far, converting healthy risk aversion into unhealthy risk *avoidance*, including an unwillingness to borrow money even for much-needed equipment or labor.

But our focus here is the benefit of low leverage, especially as related to innovation. For example, the FLP family firm, which manufactures specialty metal fabrications and holds numerous real estate entities, has a bank agreement that includes a covenant providing a debt-to-equity ratio of up to three times the debt to equity. But FLP family leaders opted to set their internal bar at two times debt to equity, reasoning that even if money is cheap, it's best to have a sizeable cushion—to take advantage of opportunities, including those related to innovation, and to weather unexpected downturns. During recessionary times, including the Great Recession of 2009–2010, this low-leverage philosophy has served FLP well, as they and many other family firms have endured these periods without breaching any covenants or needing to borrow more money.

EXPERIMENTAL TOLERANCE

Family businesses are willing to experiment. A desire to try new things, particularly in the entrepreneurial stage, is a trait found in many family business leaders.[5] That doesn't mean they take large risks or jump blindly into innovation, but rather that they may be willing to go against CONVENTIONAL THINKING, in pursuit of new products and processes. Within public companies, this experimentation is called "intrapreneurship," as embodied by employees who see and implement new ways of doing things.

New York-based Welch Allyn, a family business that manufactures medical devices, embodies an experimental approach to innovation by soliciting ideas from its customers, employees, and the public at large, as stated on the company website:[6]

> At Welch Allyn, we make new devices and products come to life through innovative ideas. Our engineers are continuously developing next generation solutions, but we know that people just like you are thinking up inventive and resourceful ideas all the time too.... In order to continue the creative cycle, we encourage you to submit your ideas to help us create products that are inspired by you to be used by you – our customers and partners.

This openness to experimentation and innovation was established by company founder William G. Allyn, and it has helped the company achieve five decades of technical advances, sales growth, and industry recognition.

FAMILY LEADERSHIP (DECISION-MAKING)

Lack of coordination can impede or even kill innovation. This well documented but underrated factor affects the performance of both family businesses and nonfamily companies[7]. However, when a family member is involved in the innovation process, the heightened awareness this brings to the process forms an advantage for family businesses. A family member offers clout and, typically, an insider level of persuasion to get through "messy" and often political development tasks like securing funds for R&D or building a quick prototype much more effectively. The presence of such champions of innovation in the family leadership is essential for family businesses. Of course, such champions require fundamental management skills to see innovation through. A good idea is almost never enough.

Matt Schad, a fourth-generation member of the family-run Nucraft Furniture Company, is a great example of an innovation proponent. The business creates high-end office furniture that is found in some of the most prestigious US law firms and government agencies. Matt worked as an attorney with a Washington, DC, law firm before joining Nucraft, where he rose through the ranks to lead new product development. Although admittedly not a designer himself, Matt has the family position, business savvy, and legal experience to maneuver new products through the organization effectively. By combining inside talent and external design support, along with his deep legal experience, Matt has created a steady stream of products that have driven revenue growth and won high-profile industry awards.

THINGS TO REMEMBER

- Family businesses are different from nonfamily firms, and many of the ways in which they are different support their ability to innovate, which in turn supports their growth and profits and the family's well-being.

- Family-business features that serve as **innovation drivers** include
  - *personal attachments* such as family bonds, customer relationships, and interfamily business connections—all of which support innovation;
  - an *incremental approach* built on exercising moderation with R&D spending and emphasizing small changes to offerings, rather than giant leaps;
  - *longer time horizons* that yield greater patience with the development time associated with innovation;
  - *shared values*, including innovation itself, with several supporting elements such as innovation-focused objectives and cross-functional visibility;
  - *low leverage*, with an emphasis on reinvesting funds back into the business—and into innovation, specifically;
  - *experimental tolerance*, or a willingness to try new things, even when that means going against the conventional (in a calculated way);
  - *family leadership* that supports innovation by generating high-value ideas and speeding the product development process.

Chapter 2

Structured Chaos: Creating a Culture of Innovation

Darryl Brown had always admired his father, Elmer's, creativity. But he was concerned it might no longer be enough to support the growth of B&B Production Systems, the company Elmer had founded over two decades earlier and still helmed as chief executive officer (CEO).

Industry leaders and observers considered Elmer Brown, now 75, a true innovator and pioneer in production automation. As proof, United States-based B&B Production Systems, the Brown family business, continued to earn most of its income from products based on the patriarch's 12 patents; these related mostly to the integration of specific electrical components into robotics and other automation devices used in manufacturing. Still, second-generation leader Darryl, now B&B's president, recognized it would be foolish to rely on these core products for the long term. In fact, competition from both domestic and foreign rivals had already begun to cut into B&B's share, and technology standards were changing at unprecedented rates in the new millennium. Moreover, competitors were succeeding with more innovative business models and organizations than B&B's.

Although Darryl was aware of these mounting challenges, Elmer was reluctant to create new applications with different or modified technologies. In addition, as a lifelong product engineer, the elder Brown had little interest in experimenting with selling and service approaches or organizational change. Luckily, Darryl had the support of other second-generation members. His brother, Jim, the company's CFO, had a clear perspective on what key numbers meant. Their cousin Will ran the main production plant with a focus on continuous quality improvement. As head of sales, Jim's wife (Darryl's sister-in-law), Nikki, was fully engaged in figuring out how to improve sales. Revenue had peaked at $110 million the previous year, then plunged 20 percent because of a market downturn and stiffening competition. Although still profitable, B&B had a much lower cash flow than in previous years, with little relief on the horizon.

Darryl and other executive team members faced multiple complex tasks in promoting B&B's growth: diversifying offerings, increasing sales channels, changing some family members' responsibilities, and most challenging, infusing a new, more innovation-focused culture into the company. The immediate challenge was that individual leaders were overwhelmed with day-to-day responsibilities, which were, ironically, heightened by digital advancements such as online customer support. As leaders spent increasing time on customer requests and other operational issues, no one was thinking about the future and the multidimensional innovations required to secure it.

Darryl himself struggled to rise above the daily routine, including his tendency to get pulled into family matters large and small. He had recently had to postpone an important dinner discussion of a new product application with B&B's largest customer in order to sit down with his sister, Beth, and brother-in-law, Carl, to discuss Carl's work behavior. The brother-in-law, who worked at the plant, had a history of alcohol abuse, and it was affecting his performance at B&B. This matter was just one of the many things interfering with Darryl's thoughts about improving innovation and culture at the business.

On the bright side, B&B's stronger operational focus also had advantages. A series of economic challenges over the past decade had sharpened the business's focus on cost reduction through process and labor-related efficiency. While this had diminished the company's focus on new product development—of great concern as sales of the main product line diminished—it had also led to an operationally focused culture featuring rapid customer response and the best on-time delivery record in the industry.

Darryl's challenge, then, was to preserve B&B's culture of operational excellence while building a strong focus on product and service innovation alongside it. Given the challenge of shifting leadership's focus from day-to-day responsibilities, he suspected he would need to secure outside assistance with design and innovation.

Late one afternoon, as Darryl was contemplating how to develop new automation products, Will came into his office to let him know that the price of copper for B&B's main product line was rising sharply. Nikki had already warned Darryl that week that any price increases were unfeasible, as their main competitors were holding firm on their prices and had even signaled possible near-term discounts. The developments made Darryl realize something important: he had to help his team engage in more innovative thinking in *all* areas of the business—from new product development, to pricing structure, to organization. Doing that meant shifting B&B's culture to be much more innovation driven. On the way home, Darryl began creating a mental list of things he could do to drive this change.

* * *

BUILDING A CULTURE OF INNOVATION: THREE KEY QUESTIONS

Developing a culture of innovation is a critical step in building and sustaining a multigeneration family firm, no matter the business's sector of focus. This is not easy. The more he thought about it, B&B president Darryl Brown understood that there is no simple definition of a culture of innovation, let alone a step-by-step process or roadmap to follow. This is partly because culture-based elements of innovation are relatively new topics of study. As such, to provide meaningful guidance on this emerging topic, this chapter will consider three important, interrelated questions.

- What is a culture of innovation?
- Why create a culture of innovation?
- How can a culture of innovation be created?

WHAT IS A CULTURE OF INNOVATION?

To create a *culture of innovation*, we must first understand each part of the phrase: culture and innovation. Broadly, the word "culture" is thought of as describing "the totality of socially transmitted behavior patterns, arts, beliefs, institutions, and all other products of human work and thought in a particular country or region of the world..."[1] But since the word entered the business lexicon in the late 1980s, it has become deeply connected with the aggregation of core values, vision, work-environment characteristics, employee interaction, industry dynamics, customer service, vendor relations, market position, and the *ability to change* that are associated with a corporation, start-up, family business, or company of any type. More directly stated, culture is the values and beliefs that define who we are and how we operate.

Beyond the general use of the culture concept in business, there is an inherent understanding that family firms demonstrate genuine cultural differences in how they function on multiple dimensions. Family firms tend to work hard to generate a company culture, while nonfamily firms may let it develop on its own or allow their culture to change based on shifting leadership or market features. Regarding the "innovation" part of the culture-of-innovation concept, of the items in the list of cultural features above, "ability to change" is most relevant. Ability to change, or adaptability, is the best indicator of a firm's culture of innovation, whether it is a family business or nonfamily company. Recall from the Introduction our definition of innovation: *creative change that produces meaningful results*. Thus, family businesses that demonstrate a proactive ability to drive meaningful, value-adding change are those with the strongest cultures of innovation.

- In some family firms, the notion of innovation, creativity, or change is clearly stated in their values, which may be posted on the walls of the company. S.C. Johnson, the global household cleaning company that uses the tag line "A family business," makes its values as clear as glass freshly cleaned by Windex®, one of its products:
    - entrepreneurship
    - innovation

- risk-taking
- knowledge and technology
- employee welfare
- customer relationship marketing
- vision
- proactivity
- global thinking[2]

According to this list, the Johnson family explicitly values innovation. Supporting innovation are the complementary values of entrepreneurship and risk-taking. It takes an entrepreneurial drive and some investment risk to make innovation real and meaningful. The four generations of Johnsons have been inspired to exemplify these values by the story of founder Samuel Curtis Johnson: at age 53, he launched a flooring company and soon diversified into floor maintenance when he observed his customers needed a product to preserve their new floors.

Most family businesses have not been as intentional or broad scope about innovation as the Johnsons. In other family firms, innovation may be exhibited mostly in one area of the business, or only for specific issue or periods of time. A family firm in the adhesive coating industrial sector discovered that one of their key ingredients was going to be discontinued by its sole supplier. Understanding that this would devastate their business, a team of engineers, managers, and salespeople banded together to generate a creative solution. It turned out that one of the salespeople's customers knew a different vendor with a similar ingredient. After some joint development with that vendor, which was also a family business, the formula was developed to suit their needs, resulting in an even better adhesive. This was just one specific time the family firm exhibited such joint problem-solving innovation. The innovative culture was not embedded in this family firm as it is in S. C. Johnson.

Creating a culture of innovation shouldn't be about product/service developments alone (although the next chapter discusses that topic in detail). On the one hand, there may be no greater practical way to create a "sense" of innovation than to produce a steady stream of new market-focused products. New-product introductions are exciting and highly visible to the organization and its stakeholders. On the other hand, to maximize performance, companies benefit from aiming for innovation on multiple levels. That means long-lasting family firms work on creative ways to

- take measured risks to develop new wealth while preserving foundational or legacy wealth;
- blend diverse family members working in the business with capable nonfamily executives;
- transition ownership from one generation to the next while balancing incentive to work hard with financial security;
- develop the next generation into leaders who are able to reinvent the business for greater growth, building upon the founder's legacy without trying to replicate the founder's hero image;
- live family values that set the tone for business continuity while remaining focused on managing a healthy business in the short term;
- steward family resources in a manner that benefits customers, employees, communities, and family members;
- develop effective governance practices that balance the sometimes conflicting needs of the family, management, and ownership.

Together, these elements define and support a highly innovative family business culture.

It is also important to point out the *paradoxical*, or yin-yang, nature of a culture of innovation, especially in a family business.[3] For example, family business expert John L. Ward notes how the long-standing Italian family firm Beretta, maker of firearms, has a culture and practices that reflect its company motto: "Prudence and audacity." In essence, the Beretta family values *both* prudently caring for the family business's ongoing health *and* acting audaciously to innovate into new areas of potential growth. In a *Harvard Business Review* article on growth, Rita Gunther McGrath reinforces this notion, concluding that companies need to devote adequate focus to their core businesses to provide stability, while dedicating sufficient resources to drive relevant innovation.[4] Thus the highest-performing family firms tend to be those that balance careful decision-making and a focus on continuity (prudence and stability) with bold but healthy risk-taking (audacity and innovation).

The theme of paradox in cultures of innovation is also related to the idea of *ambidexterity*.[5] That is, family firms that can both exploit existing resources (e.g., focus on efficiency enhancement) and explore new opportunities (e.g. focus on effectiveness enhancement, including through innovation) tend to deliver better performance than those that can't. While B&B, the family firm in our opening example, had built strong exploitation capabilities through operational excellence, Darryl and other second-generation leaders wanted to increase the business's focus on exploration through continuous innovation or change.

So, family leaders who are looking to build a culture of innovation must become comfortable with managing the paradoxes of prudence and audacity, stability and change, and exploitation and exploration, becoming more ambidextrous through ambition, vision, focus, and experience. That means routinely stepping out of their comfort zones to take calculated risks on multiple elements. The reward of their efforts could be a true culture of innovation that facilitates creativity at all levels of the business, thus enabling fast adaptation to shifts in demand and competition.

WHY CREATE A CULTURE OF INNOVATION?

A 2007 Bain and Company study shows that the average life expectancy of US companies is only ten years, and that the profitable life of the average product has dropped 70 percent in the past decade.[6] All businesses today, including family firms, face unprecedented challenges, including the pace of market change. Macroeconomic trends are driving a growing need for faster, more pervasive innovation in product and service offerings, geographic expansion and go-to-market strategies, as suggested by Robert Cooper in his book *Winning at New Products*.[7] Among the specific trends Cooper cites are exponential advances in technology, fast-changing customer needs, a fourfold decrease in product life cycles in the last

50 years, and increased globalization (which expands both opportunity and threat).

Along with these changes, family firms in sectors like hardware and grocery are struggling to compete with large public companies or private-equity-owned firms that have the financial and strategic prowess to roll up significant segments of a whole industry, capturing large market shares while putting smaller competitors out of business. Foreign competitors with much lower prices, including those from China, have also entered many markets, as suggested by the mention of globalization above. The Internet now provides unprecedented price transparency and the promise of hyper-fast delivery. In addition, changes in estate tax rates and other legislation in the U.S. have made ownership succession more complex for family firms.

Creating a family business culture of innovation can help structure and overcome this accelerating pace and mounting chaos, enabling the enterprise to generate fast, creative solutions throughout the family business. As the underlying foundation for the family business, an innovation-focused culture should pervade all areas of the organization and the family—not just as related to products/services. The FBCG's deep experience with multigeneration family firm clients suggests that those companies with a holistic innovative culture maximize their odds of long-term continuity. In short, *a culture of continuous innovation promotes family business continuity*, enabling the family to maintain long-term ownership, providing opportunities for next-generation members, and strengthening the wealth and welfare of the extended family.

Hopefully, it's clear by now that even with all the right strategic intentions, high performance is difficult to achieve consistently without the right culture. Just to drive that point home further, consider contrasting examples. Byrne Electrical Specialists, a family business cited in chapter 1, manufactures and installs power outlets in furniture, airport counters, and many other sites. As the company's website states, "Byrne Electrical Specialists has always been an innovator."[8] In line with this, Byrne family leaders take pride in the fact that their original patented products, which once represented 100 percent of sales, now make up less than 60 percent, with the growth of new products outpacing that of established ones. The business has carefully created new products to fit trends in globalization (specifically, outlets that can handle plugs from multiple countries). Byrne has also innovated with regard to order management and other areas, including the development of an on-site daycare facility—Wee Folk—for the children of employees and those of other community families. These innovative actions have inspired customers and employees alike, while maintaining strong sales and profits over two generations.

Compare Byrne to an example of a family business that failed to embrace change with a culture of innovation. For decades, the bicycle manufacturer Schwinn dominated U.S. sales as a much-loved household name. But over time the Chicago-based family firm focused excessively on processes, procedures, and maintenance of the status quo, at the expense of much-needed product innovation and management changes.[9] By the time Schwinn recognized the need to shift from bulky but well-crafted bikes to more affordable, lighter-weight, multisprocket products like mountain bicycles, it had missed a critical window of opportunity and was poorly equipped to make new products in its outdated factory. The business went bankrupt in 1992.

In general, family firms that stop innovating and move into protection mode—playing *not to lose* rather than playing to win—will quickly decline in the market. That said, some family firms have been able to bounce back after long periods with suboptimal culture. Ford, still a family-controlled firm, had thrown all its resources at right-sizing the operation in the new millennium, while ignoring the development of new products.[10] It took the courage and vision of the family chairman and a fourth-generation member, Bill Ford, to go outside the industry and recruit an innovative thinker from Boeing. President and CEO Alan Mulally has infused Ford with a new culture that includes transparency and innovation, taking the iconic company from the brink of bankruptcy to unprecedented profits, fueled by innovative products and management practices.

So it's never too late to aim for a culture of innovation to have an impact.

HOW CAN A CULTURE OF INNOVATION BE CREATED?

As we have seen, a family business culture of innovation represents the convergence of multiple factors. FBCG's database and outside research suggest these are the main ingredients:

1. **Start at the Top**—Without real family leadership and support, there is minimal chance of creating an innovative culture. It is common for family leaders to go through the struggles Darryl Brown is experiencing at B&B. He knows he needs to shift the company's culture and mind-set, and he knows he's the one who must lead the change, because other leaders are overburdened by the demands of day-to-day business needs. At both family and nonfamily firms, one of the main responsibilities of the CEO is to set the enterprise's tone and culture. For a family business, establishing a strong culture (including innovation) is at least as important as achieving shareholder returns, protecting family assets, creating a strategic business plan, and building a strong management team.

2. **Go Incremental**—A series of smaller developments versus major breakthroughs is more likely to ensure long-term success in a family business. Family firms that hit singles are more likely to survive and thrive than those that consistently swing for the fences. Singles produce more runs.[11] As the leader of B&B, Darryl's goal was not to develop a whole new set of patents like his father's, but rather to make smaller scale but meaningful changes to existing product lines and to establish line extensions that kept the company relevant and strong in the market. That formula has worked very well for players in the automotive industry, where for decades multiple small-component innovations have created a much better overall product—the modern automobile. This same formula can work for family businesses.

3. **Be Outcome Driven (But Don't Micromanage)**—Instead of being concerned only with the details of how an initiative is going to be accomplished, strong family business leaders should focus on clearly envisioning and discussing outcomes with multiple groups

in the business, to help paint the picture of the desired outcome and inspire people to work toward it.[12] In short, don't micromanage, but do hold teams accountable for meaningful progress—as long as the vision is clear. At Byrne Electrical Specialists, family leaders set a clear goal of developing a new type of electrical outlet for office furniture, then empowered their engineers and designers to find the best route to creating it.

4. **Define Innovation as Positive Change**—Change is hard, but necessary. Not surprisingly, calls for organizational change will usually result in resistance. So it's up to leaders to explain the motivation and goals for a shift to a culture of innovation, especially by framing these in a positive light and helping drive creative problem solving across areas. Early results should then help promote greater acceptance.

5. **Promote Trust**—Mistakes and failures pave the path to a culture of innovation and will continue to occur in any innovative organization. While "celebrate failures" and "fail fast and move on" are popular buzz phrases today, the real key to success is creating an environment where people are willing to act creatively without fear of reprisal, as opposed to remaining passive to avoid mistakes. Promoting a trusting environment that rewards *calculated* risk-taking in service of innovation is paramount and will support a willingness to experiment in all areas of the business.

6. **Seek Innovative Board Members**—Selecting board members who are innovative themselves (as proven in their careers) and willing to ask provocative questions about products, processes, and other potential innovations will help develop and support change-oriented thinking at the top governance level. We have consistently observed the presence of innovation-minded board members in successful family firms across sectors. One strategy, as demonstrated by the earlier Ford Motor Company example, is to seek board members with innovative experience in industries outside the family business's sector of focus, in order to bring fresh thinking/perspective to the firm.

7. **Make Space**—Making space for innovation literally means creating the right physical environment to nurture new ideas. There is a whole set of books and other material devoted to developing

optimal spaces for innovation, including those that derive lessons from innovation giants like Google and Pixar.[13] Any family business in any sector can create more innovation-friendly space and processes. Steelcase and other leading office furniture manufacturers, for example, have found that capturing more outside light, creating open spaces, offering ease of data sharing, and developing collaborative furniture can greatly enhance outcome-driven creativity.

HOW THEY DID IT

Now that we've defined a culture of innovation and considered why and how to develop one, let's consider how several family firms exemplify such a culture, inspiring creativity at all organizational levels. The following list highlights features of a culture of innovation from real family businesses, along several diverse scopes.

- **Balancing stability with innovation**—Pablo had an ambitious vision. The newly minted MBA had just joined his family's business, a Mexico-based food equipment manufacturer. Based on his previous experience with building materials giant Cemex and his MBA training, Paolo was eager to help the family firm expand to other countries in the Americas, Europe, and Asia, using innovative go-to-market strategies (including low initial pricing). Paolo's father, Hernando, the 75-year-old CEO and chair, liked the idea of global expansion, but felt his son's vision might be too risky. Specifically, Hernando felt a strong obligation to continue providing dividends and the promise of a healthy inheritance to his other five children, especially the three who did not work with the business. After much discussion, the family together agreed to approach international expansion over a longer time period, while developing a clear dividend policy stipulating the amount of funds available for new business development. They set a percentage range of net operating income for "innovative investment in new business," including within overseas markets, and for payout of dividends.

Their staged approach balanced stability (strong dividends, assets) and innovation (growth through new markets and strategies).

- **Optimizing leadership**—At a Pennsylvania-based automotive supplier, the family owners have built a culture of collaborative problem solving and support to grow their thermo plastics product lines and businesses. But it hasn't been easy. Hired into the business some years ago was an outside executive who turned out to have an excessive focus on individual product line growth and profits. This senior manager's influence shifted the firm's mentality toward short-term results, silo-based thinking, and the maximization of profits at all costs. Once the family patriarch saw the diminished spirit of collaborative innovation, he made an immediate leadership change, replacing the executive in question and creating a new role for a family member to oversee cross-business sharing of ideas and practices. This helped the firm return quickly to its culture of shared value creation.
- **Transitioning ownership**—At a family-owned fuel and convenience store business, the two second-generation sibling leaders wished to transition ownership to the third generation. They knew that simply gifting the business to their children was too risky, as their own retirement relied on ongoing income from the firm. At the same time, the third generation couldn't afford to pay the net book value for the business, as that would have left them without sufficient cushion or capital. Working closely with their tax advisor and attorney, the two generations crafted a unique shareholder agreement that included a combination of gifting and purchasing over a ten-year period. The senior generation retained ownership of the firm's two main buildings for the decade in question, and would receive lease payments for that period. Moreover, half the business shares were gifted, and the other half were sold at a discounted rate. The innovative agreement secured the outgoing generation's retirement, while ensuring the incoming owners reasonable capital and debt levels.
- **Developing the next generation**—The Rawling family, owners of a trucking company, have a creative family employment provision. Along with the common family business requirement of a college

degree and at least three years of outside work experience, the family specifies that members interested in joining the business must first *start or acquire their own business,* independently or as part of the broader family firm. The young family member must, at minimum, submit a business plan for the start-up or acquisition. A committee then decides whether to approve funding. Funded projects receive support through a family venture fund and guidance from one of the nonfamily executives. This innovative requirement exposes the upcoming generation to the many dimensions of diversifying the family business, preparing them to take on future challenges as family business employees.

- **Leveraging governance bodies**—The Chevy Chase Land Company was founded by Senator Francis G. Newlands in 1890. Now in its fourth and fifth generation, the enterprise has over 100 family shareholders. The family created a family council to facilitate communications among the family shareholders, board, and management. No passive body, the family council has been pivotal in creating education programs for a broad range of shareholders (especially upcoming generations) and developing better communication mechanisms among the three constituent groups, ensuring greater harmony across the enterprise.

The list above makes clear there are many different ways to develop and maintain a culture of innovation. Subsequent chapters touch on many of these in more detail. To return to our example of innovation at B&B Production Systems, after much contemplation and discussion of ideas with fellow second-generation leaders, Darryl Brown implemented a list of high-potential items to move the company toward a more innovative culture; many of the items reflect the ideas discussed earlier.

- **Symbols, Stories, and Messages**
  - *Visual reminders*—The leaders framed and displayed all patents in the entrance lobby, along with a timeline showing when key products had been developed/introduced, to symbolize B&B's strong tradition of innovation and inspire employees to carry this on.

- *Organizing principles*—Darryl worked with his team to develop the rallying principle of "**Structured chaos**," which encouraged managers and employees to balance stability and innovation in promoting growth.
- Education and Communication
  - *Knowledge building*—Management made innovation-focused articles and books available to all employees and started a book/article study group that met regularly and rotated leadership of discussion. Darryl also joined a regional new product development association to gain insights into best practices.
  - *Communications*—B&B held several company meetings to explain the need for greater innovation and communicate the idea that both successes and failures would be celebrated, as long as they resulted in some form of growth/learning.
- Talent and Teams
  - *Job descriptions and performance plans*—The team rewrote key leaders' job descriptions and individual performance plans to focus more sharply on supporting and promoting innovation.
  - *Outside support*—B&B hired an independent designer to work closely with the team on the next line of products. Management also assigned an innovation-minded engineer to guide the relationship.
  - *Cross-functional teams*—Management created high-level cross-functional teams to stimulate creative thinking about new product and service development.
- Financial
  - *Innovation-focused revenue analysis and goals*—The team analyzed and shared the amount of revenue attributable to new products, setting ambitious goals to increase this proportion over time.
  - *Innovation budget*—The company created multiple, differentiated line items in the budget to pay for innovation.
  - *Variable compensation*—B&B began to tie a percentage of new product sales into the bonus program.

- **Process**
  - *Formal innovation process*—Management started formalizing a B&B innovation process (see Product and Service Innovation chapter 3 for details on how do this).
  - *Channeling the voice of the customer*—B&B became more deliberate about listening to the customer by conducting surveys and using the data secured to inform creation of new products.

BEWARE THESE PITFALLS

Family businesses that are seeking to create a culture of innovation should take a thoughtful approach. That includes avoiding specific pitfalls we've observed, such as the ones below.

- **Sacrificing operations for innovation**—The Bolum family business, which manufactures automotive parts, was so excited about incorporating innovation into their culture that family leaders took their eye off the core businesses that were providing the means to be more innovative in the first place. Luckily, they recognized this misstep before sales AND margins declined significantly. From that point on, they emphasized innovation across the board, including for the core business. That meant improving processes, modifying products, and developing new human resources (HR) policies for ongoing business, while also thinking creatively about new product development, acquisitions, and joint ventures.
- **Sacrificing innovation for operations**—This is the flip side to the pitfall above. Too many family businesses find themselves unable to make space for innovation because they are caught up in running the core business. B&B, our main example in this chapter, illustrates this challenge well: family leaders were so focused on managing day-to-day customer and family issues that they had minimal time to think about longer-term innovation. Had they remained unable to promote innovation, the business's performance would have suffered.

- **Nurturing the naysayers**—"You know it will never fly," one of the Wright brothers' business neighbors in Ohio used to say regularly of their prototype airplanes. Innovators of any type will always face doubt, from others and themselves, whether the doubters call themselves devil's advocates, doubting Thomases, or caring colleagues. While there's always a place for constructive critique, family firms with too many naysayers or those who make too much room for doubt will likely fail to innovate. One business family has a mantra-like guideline for deemphasizing doubt to create a more innovative mind-set: "Don't focus on excuses ('No, because...'). Do focus on possibilities ('Yes, IF...')." *No*, this contraption will not fly *because* the material is too heavy. Or the positive, innovative mind-set: *yes*, this contraption will fly *if* we find the right material that is light enough and strong enough.

THINGS TO REMEMBER

- Family businesses that develop strong cultures of innovation are more likely to enjoy improved performance on all levels for the long term.
- *What is a culture of innovation?* A culture of innovation is embodied in an environment that encourages and supports a proactive ability to drive meaningful, value-added change on multiple dimensions, such as with regard to new products and services, ownership transition, and governance practices. Strong cultures of innovation tend to have paradoxical features, such as their support of both stability and change.
- *Why create a culture of innovation?* As competition mounts and the average lifespan of a company and product drops, it's important to find ways to boost growth and longevity. Multiple examples support the idea that a culture of continuous innovation will promote family business continuity.
- *How can a culture of innovation be created?* Multiple mutually reinforcing factors can help promote a culture of innovation, including leadership

and board support, a focus on incremental change, and the promotion of trust. Successful family businesses develop these success factors through symbols and messages, education, communication, talent, and process changes.
- *Pitfalls* on the way to a culture of innovation include overemphasis on operations or innovation (at the expense of the other) and an excessive focus on naysaying.

Chapter 3

New Products and Services: Driving Value with Innovative Offerings

"What should we do?" That was the question on Howard Tuthill's mind as he walked through his family's factory one cold winter afternoon in 1930. The grease-laden cast iron machine tools surrounding Howard shone in dim sunlight. Only a handful of the workstations were occupied, making the cavernous space much quieter than in recent years, a sign of the challenging situation the business faced.

Oliver Machinery Company, the Tuthills' family business, had been launched in 1890 with the introduction of an innovative, labor-saving wood trimmer. The firm had expanded quickly to offer a full range of woodworking equipment—saws, planers, sanders, lathes, and drills—to satisfy a steadily increasing stream of orders, mostly from premier furniture makers. But with the onset of the Great Depression in 1929, business had slowed to a crawl, and it was no longer clear Oliver could survive.

Evidence of the downturn was everywhere. Leaving the factory, Howard walked downtown and saw people waiting in line at the local YMCA for free meals. He watched as government officials ladled out soup to each person and tore pieces of bread from large loaves. As he walked away, Howard pictured two seemingly disparate images: bread being torn from a loaf and saw blades cutting through a piece of wood.

"That's it!" Howard blurted to himself. He raced back to the factory and began designing a new product: the first commercial bread slicer. Fast-forward to modern times, when bread-slicing machines are ubiquitous, used by 80 percent of U.S. supermarket bakeries and most retail bakeries, such as Panera Bread.

The next two generations of the Tuthill family continued diversifying the company into new areas, including bread packaging, labeling, medical device packaging, and specialty food service equipment. The Tuthills exemplify an important segment of innovation in a family business: creating profitable new products and services.

* * *

NEW PRODUCTS AND SERVICES: THE LARGEST AREA OF FAMILY BUSINESS INNOVATION

The lifeblood of a family business is providing competitive, differentiated offerings that customers want or need, sometimes even before they know they want them. In fact, much of a family's enterprise value can be traced to the successful development and commercialization of novel products and services over time.

It is easy to find examples of such creativity. As noted above, the Tuthill family firm emerged from the Great Depression by offering a new, mechanized technology for slicing bread. Bakers immediately saw the value of the innovation, as it would reduce their labor costs while increasing their output of saleable product. The Tuthills built on the bread slicer's success by developing other innovative bakery and food service products, as well as products outside of these areas, driving the business's growth over time.

Similarly, family firms across sectors use innovation, often technology driven, to create offerings. For instance, the current generation of the Custer family, which designs office environments and sells office furniture, has developed a digital rendering service for clients who wish to envision a new space or need digitally produced and enhanced photography for promotion material. This new service offering has quickly contributed to the family firm's cash flow. Even Oliver's rather low-tech original bread slicer was morphed by the family into an adjustable-thickness slicer that uses advanced servo drives to control the thickness setting. Any such technology-driven improvements result from a strong focus on and execution of innovation.

Given the importance of new product and service development, this activity receives the majority of family business innovation resources, as the figure 3.1 suggests. Specifically, FBCG advisors surveyed noted that their clients who consistently exhibited innovative or entrepreneurial behavior focused most innovative efforts on developing new products, services, or ventures.[1]

Interestingly, the survey also showed a good balance of innovation efforts in other areas of the family business, including those related to ownership structure and succession. This supports a fundamental premise of this book, that innovation in family business is not just about developing new products and services, and that the most successful firms draw on innovation across multiple dimensions.

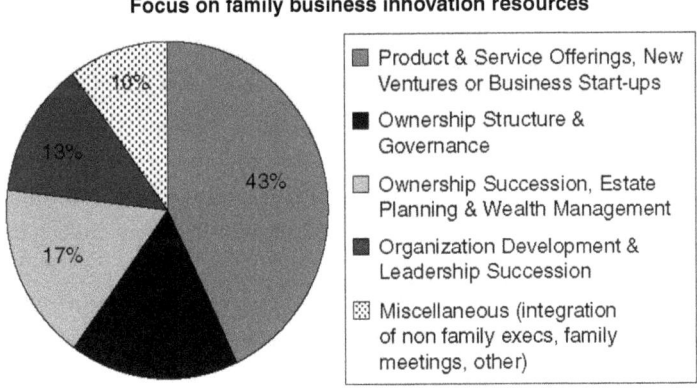

FIGURE 3.1 Focus of family business innovation resources

DRIVERS OF PRODUCT/SERVICE INNOVATION IN FAMILY BUSINESS

As discussed in chapter 1 on "Family Business Differences," several "drivers" help promote innovation within family businesses. Closely aligned with those drivers are those factors that relate directly to product/service innovation:

- customer and supplier relationships
- controlled risk-taking
- incremental developments
- low leverage
- longer-term horizon

The following subsections dive more deeply into each of these drivers.

Customer and Supplier Relationships

Because of their close, often personal connection with customers and other partners, family businesses can receive early signals as to what the market wants or needs—often to a greater extent than nonfamily firms might. In product development, this element of proximity is often more vital than the presence of a brilliant technical manager or employee, as suggested by Frank Bacon and Thomas Butler in their book *Planned Innovation*: "The gift-of-genius myth asserts that all you have to do to succeed with new products is to find the right person and give him or her time to invent products. However, even if such a highly qualified genius is found, the products produced are usually doomed to failure because it does not emphasize the critical importance of developing products or services which meet the market needs or wants."[2] Family firms' deep relationships help them understand market needs more fully.

Part of the benefit for family firms is that being close to customers and suppliers often leads to the participation of these groups in the development and testing of new offerings. Back when the Tuthills' Oliver Products Company was moving into the medical device packaging market, a key customer (Critikon, a division of Johnson & Johnson) and supplier (DuPont) were instrumental in helping the firm develop a new form of packaging. They worked with Oliver engineers to add a coating that could withstand the pressure of ethylene oxide sterilization to Dupont's Tyvek material—a key component in the packaging Oliver made. That innovation helped Oliver customers like Critikon ensure their physician and nurse end users that every package sold to them contained a sterile device (in this case, a catheter). Family firms' close customer and supplier relationships provide highly valuable inputs for profitable innovation.

Controlled Risk-taking

Both family and nonfamily firms take risks. Research suggests that family firms, compared to nonfamily firms, tend to take fewer risks or focus on "safer" risks that are closely associated with their core business.[3] Such observation has led to the myth that family firms are *risk averse*. In reality, because family firms demonstrate superior performance over the long run, it could be argued that they actually take more "high-probability" risks than nonfamily firms. A *McKinsey Quarterly* article shows that family firms outperformed a broader public company index over a ten-year period.[4] As discussed earlier, family firms may rarely "bet the farm" or "go all in" on innovation; rather, they take a conservative, calculated approach to risk-taking, including risks related to innovation, that appear to deliver higher value over the long term.

Oliver's enterprise value grew as the family took successive low-level risks that allowed them to move into new markets with modified products. Cutting and sawing technology for wood led to creative applications in bread slicing, which motivated the Tuthills to target bakeries as customers. In turn, the need to store sliced bread led to the development of packaging equipment for bakeries and other food processors, and the seal Oliver created for the original wax paper packaging material was modified into labels that served the dual purpose of holding the material together and identifying the product. Further, the adhesive used on the labels contributed to the development of medical device packaging that provided ethylene oxide sterilization. Thus each product innovation built logically upon a previous one, resulting in a diverse set of offerings that required less risk than developing each product from scratch.

Incremental Developments

New product and service developments in a family business, particularly after the first generation, tend to build upon the core offering, as exemplified by the Oliver story. Most family businesses aren't going to win "Most Innovative" awards in business publications, at least not as measured by new product and service introductions. These are mainly the domain of high-growth venture-capital-backed players like the early Google, or of the well-established, well-funded R&D departments of large public firms like Proctor & Gamble or General Electric.

Yet family businesses excel at producing a steady stream of new offerings that represent extensions of current products and services. That's in part because family businesses tend to conduct frequent small-scale experiments, according to family business advisor John L. Ward: "We call this proactive adaptability.... because [family businesses] tend to have vertical integration and more diversification, they are constantly sensing and testing new ideas all around themselves. Because continuity is the purpose, with prudence as the governor, they make lots of little experiments all the time. They develop the ability to be adaptable, deliberately."[5] This adaptability helps fuel successful product and service innovation.

Even Cargill, considered the largest privately held family business in the U. S., grew into a multibillion-dollar multinational mainly by expanding through its core market area of agriculture. According to the book *Grow from Within*, "[Cargill's] founding business was a grain elevator near a railroad track, then it began trading commodities, then it went into the primary transformation businesses (e.g., turning soybeans into protein, oils, and so on), which led into businesses such as animal feed and basic food supplies."[6] Each of these incremental growth extensions required some level of innovation to sustain Cargill as a successful family firm now over 150 years in operation.

The Kohler Company is another family firm that has used continuous product innovation to thrive. One focus of the firm's innovation is what might be considered a very basic commodity: the bathtub. As the family story goes, the first Kohler bath, made from a cast iron horse trough, sold in 1883 for one cow and 14 chickens! The four Kohler generations have continuously combined form and function, or what they call "beauty and practicality," to develop a wide array of kitchen and bath products for home and commercial settings. Product offerings range from contemporary kitchen plumbing fixtures to the most advanced toilet and bidet systems (with automatic lid-closing technology, of course). Perhaps just as visionary and creative is Kohler's long-term view: "Working toward sustainability is an ongoing journey for Kohler, and creating water-conserving products has been a key component since the 1970's...[We have] a global sustainability goal of net zero and a strategy to reduce and offset our environmental footprint every year until we reach that goal by 2035."[7] This vision helps drive Kohler's innovation, a process that is more evolutionary than groundbreaking.

Low Leverage

Family firms take conservative financial approaches to each element of their businesses, including those related to developing new offerings. This creates a resourceful mind-set or culture that is found throughout the family business landscape. In fact, research has shown that *parsimony* is one of three characteristics of family governance that distinguish family firms from other organizational forms.[8] Parsimony refers to the propensity of family firms to be vigilant about their financial resources, largely because these are personally owned resources. This frugal mentality, when practiced in moderation, actually underscores the drive for families to be more prudent with the use of their limited resources, including vis-à-vis innovation. In chapter 1 on "Family Business Differences," we discussed how a family-owned specialty metal fabrication firm set an internal bar that limited their debt-to-equity ratio to two, although the bank's stated maximum was three. That approach provided a good cushion to both capitalize on innovation opportunities and weather downturns such as the 2009 recession.

Longer-term Horizon

Having a longer-term horizon means that most family firms are able to withstand the pressures of having to earn a quick return on investment. That suggests, in turn, that while pushing to develop and launch new offerings, family businesses are more tolerant of delays and more understanding of the time extra iterations may take. This helps them turn out high-quality, innovative products without rushing. It took Kohler years to develop a reliable porcelain tub.

INNOVATION PROCESSES

Each family business starts with an idea and grows with new ones. The ideas are often about a product that the market needs, like bread—a basic food staple—or variations of the product, such as whole-grain bread. The Tuthill family firm started with the idea of developing a wood trimmer to help the crews of lumber barons cut timber. Over time, the firm developed new woodworking equipment and machinery to enable lumber yards to transform logs into buildable lumber more effectively, then leveraged this knowledge into expanding an array of other products. A steady stream of new, applicable ideas that have been developed carefully will keep any business healthy and growing. For family businesses, new ideas may ensure the firm will create revenue and employment opportunities for generations to come.

But good ideas aren't enough. The most successful firms typically have a disciplined *process* for capturing, prioritizing, developing, and commercializing these ideas, to maximize their value. The development of Howard Tuthill's bread-slicing idea followed a loosely structured process, but subsequent advancements at Oliver followed a much more disciplined approach called Planned Innovation, one of the processes described in the subsections below. This is a common pattern: processes in the founding/entrepreneurial stage tend to be less formal than in subsequent stages or generations, when the firm creates and follows multiple policies and procedures across areas of the business. For the Tuthill family, the adjustable-width slicer—which could cut thick Texas toast or ultra-thin deli meat slices—followed a new product development process that clearly identified the unmet needs of customers and guided the path to market introduction.

Much of the new product development literature today addresses various approaches to the process of product and service innovation for any kind of business, whether family owned or not. It's helpful to review selected innovation approaches to determine the advantages and variations of these as they relate to family firms. The implementation in any of the following processes, or some combination tailored to your family business, will significantly improve the odds of creating commercially successful products and services.

The Stage-Gate New Product Process

Popularized initially by Robert Cooper, the Stage-Gate process emphasizes milestones that must be achieved prior to passing through successive "toll-gates."[9] The process follows a sequential path, making it easy to understand and apply, as suggested by the figure 3.2.

As a result of the straightforward approach of this process, family firms worldwide adopted a form of the Stage-Gate process soon after it was established, even though it was not as clearly iterative as other processes that were available. Over the past two decades, Cooper and his disciples have enhanced the Stage-Gate process with more sophisticated models that include greater iteration and expanded processes within each stage, resulting in a highly robust product innovation approach. One downside is that the process has become more complicated overall, and thus may not fit all businesses' needs. But the more sophisticated Stage-Gate processes have been implemented successfully by many large well-known public firms, including DuPont, Exxon, Procter & Gamble, and Corning.

WinOvations

WinOvations[10] is an enhanced product development process built upon the previously cited process called Planned Innovation.[11] Both processes link strategic planning with new product development, leveraging the intersection of four key domains: market requirements, physical requirements, economic requirements, and resource requirements.

The WinOvations approach to new product development focuses specifically on (a) choosing the right people, (b) providing the right coaching, and (c) using the right process. Thus it emphasizes the *people* part of innovation to a greater degree than most other processes do, in order to execute the process described in figure 3.3.

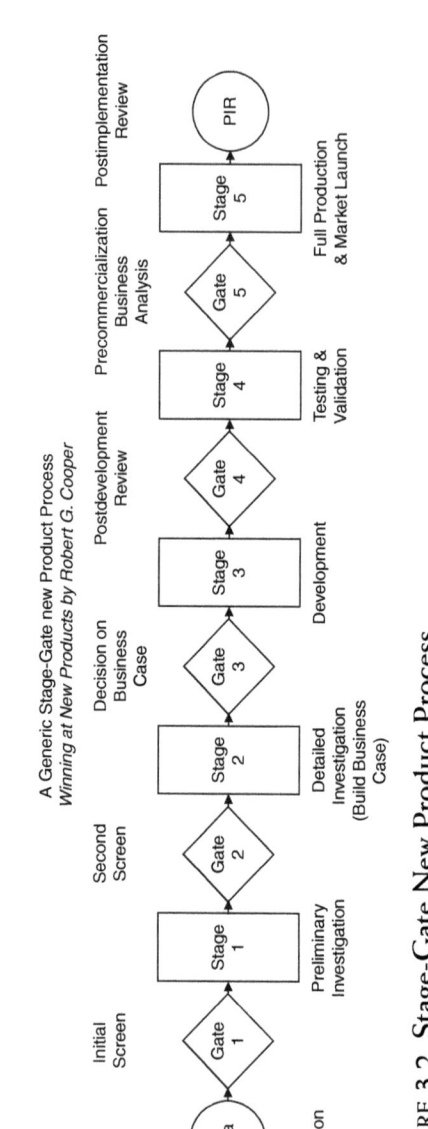

FIGURE 3.2 Stage-Gate New Product Process
www.stage-gate.com

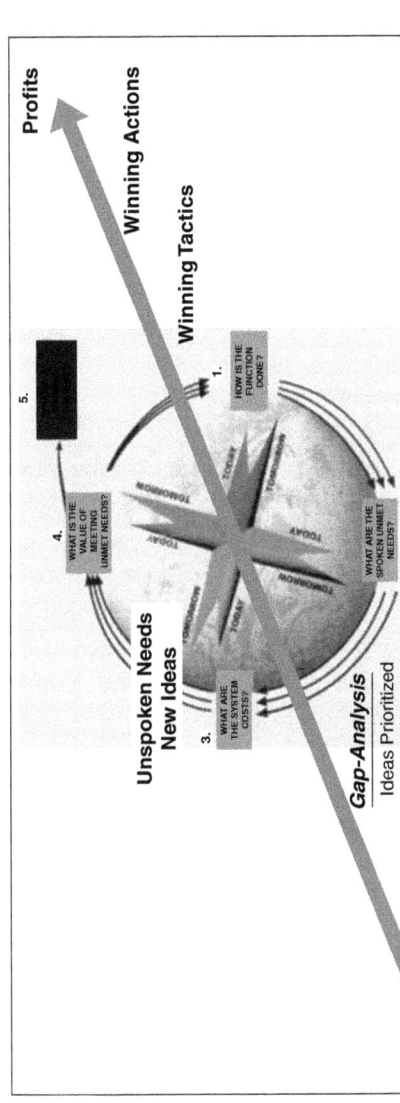

FIGURE 3.3 WinOvations New Product Development Process
www.winovations.com

Greg Stevens, the former Dow Chemical engineer who created WinOvations, researched the characteristics of people with the strongest track record for producing market valued products. His studies showed that product development "rainmakers" displayed relatively equal levels of two traits on the Myers-Briggs Type Indicator (MBTI) personality test: Intuition and Thinking (or "NT," in Myers-Briggs terms).[12] People with the highest levels of both traits could have the creativity of an artist and the analytical skills of an engineer—such as Leonardo da Vinci or, more recently, Steve Jobs. Such individuals tend to have a stronger capability to conceive of innovative products, and thus figure heavily in the "choosing the right people" part of the WinOvations approach. In fact, much of the early stage of the WinOvations process involves identifying such rainmakers and recruiting them for new product development.

Because the process of successfully innovating new offerings can be daunting, subsequent stages of WinOvations offer coaching to help rainmakers transform innovative ideas into prototypes and, ultimately, into final products. The coaching includes training rainmakers in business development and helping them follow a more disciplined process for turning inspiration into profitable offerings. Also, because most future family business leaders tend to be stronger in one area than the other—iNtuition or Thinking—additional training in the less-dominant area can be quite valuable.

Family businesses have found many elements of the WinOvations model useful. The Oliver Products Company used the "unspoken needs" step in the model's "Success Wheel" to understand that customers don't always know exactly what they need as far as new products. The Tuthills used this insight to conduct more in-depth end user research and more elaborate trend analysis to help tease out the real drivers for a new product. Through this process they understood that while Safeway's in-store bakery department explicitly asked for slicers that could provide customers with different thicknesses of bread, end-consumers' unspoken need was to have the bread sliced on-site, in front of them, so they could see the freshness firsthand. This led Oliver to develop a self-adjusting slicer that consumers could set and safely operate themselves in-store.

Design Thinking

IDEO, a well-known design firm, was founded in Silicon Valley in 1991 as the merger of four design-focused organizations, including one run by Stanford University professor David Kelley.[13] The firm has created over 5,000 innovations, including the first Apple mouse. While design firms tend to focus on more creative and aesthetic product features, they can drive very real innovation on multiple levels. Many of them achieve this using a core innovation model called "design thinking."

According to IDEO president and CEO Tim Brown, "[Design thinking] brings together what is desirable from a human point of view with what is technologically feasible and economically viable. It also allows people who aren't trained as designers to use creative tools to address a vast range of challenges."[14] IDEO applies the concepts of this designer-oriented approach to ways of thinking about new products and services. The company tries to keep the process simple, based originally on the following phases:

> Observation → Brainstorming → Rapid Prototyping → Refining → Implementation

In this way, IDEO has designed a thinking process at the intersection of the human, business, and technical spheres.

The A-to-F Method for Innovation Success

The A-to-F innovation approach was developed by marketing guru Philip Kotler and Fernando Trias De Bes to provide a systematic framework enabling innovation at any level of the organization.[15] Figure 3.4 depicts the approach.

According to Kotler and Trias De Bes, "The A-to-F Model is a step-by-step process for developing a culture of innovation, bringing together the different individuals and groups across the organization for ideas to

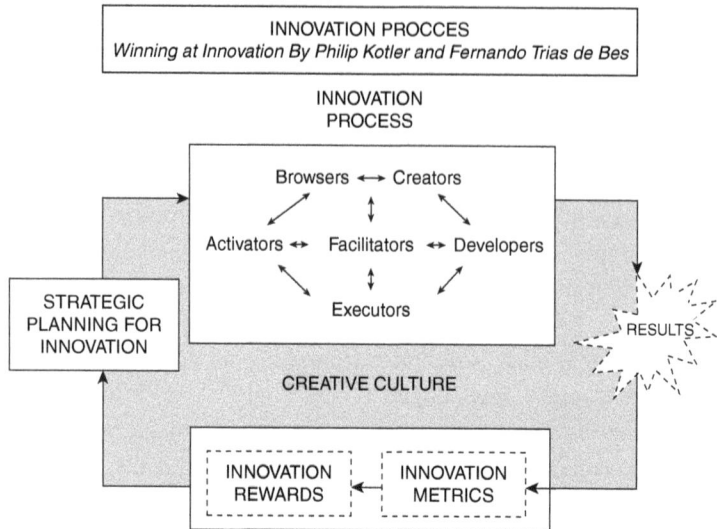

FIGURE 3.4 A-to-F Method for Innovation Success
www.innovationexcellence.com

be created, developed and implemented. Offering flexibility, the model allows a back and forth flow of ideas and creativity to adapt to changing circumstances."[16]

The A-to-F model is not actually an innovation process in the way that the others discussed in this chapter are. Rather, it is a list of key *roles* that the authors have seen at the companies they observe as exemplifying innovation practices in recent times. Their model is based on the idea that to innovate successfully, companies should assign key roles to specific individuals, then establish goals, resources, and deadlines before encouraging the individuals involved to create their own innovation process. The A-to-F roles in question are

- A: *Activators*—those who *initiate* the innovation process, with less focus on stages or outcomes;
- B: *Browsers*—search experts dedicated to providing the group with highly relevant *information* related to ideas and process;
- C: *Creators*—the *idea* producers, those who search for new solutions;

- *D: Developers*—people highly capable of *turning ideas into real offerings*, including as supported by an early-stage marketing plan;
- *E: Executors*—those trusted with *implementation*, to shepherd the innovation through the organization, to market;
- *F: Facilitators*—this role handles *management* of the innovation process, including the securing of financial and other resources as needed.

This framework and list of roles can fit nicely with family businesses because family firms tend to be highly focused on developing effective cultures, yet often need guidance to set clear roles, especially for family member executives, managers, and employees. In fact, placing family members in key roles can enhance the odds of successful, timely innovation, as discussed earlier in the book.

THE MVA INNOVATION FRAMEWORK IN FAMILY BUSINESS

As FBCG advisors, we have observed that the family firms that have a stronger track record of innovation typically follow some process, often one that reflects multiple elements of the processes and systems described above. Many families customize a specific innovation process for their use, depending on their sector of business, backgrounds of family members and executives, and preferred work styles. While there is no one "right answer" to developing an innovation process, we have observed firms succeed by following a version of the Market Value Added (MVA) Innovation Framework. The system has emerged over the past several decades as an integrative process that helps family businesses apply a more disciplined approach to innovation. Figure 3.5 illustrates the MVA Innovation Framework.

Stage 1—**Planning**—Set key strategic Objectives
Stage 2—**Screening**—Identify and screen ideas
Stage 3—**Developing**—Design/test/prototype the concept
Stage 4—**Marketing**—Prepare the market and organization for product production and sales
Stage 5—**Launching**—Propel the offering into the marketplace

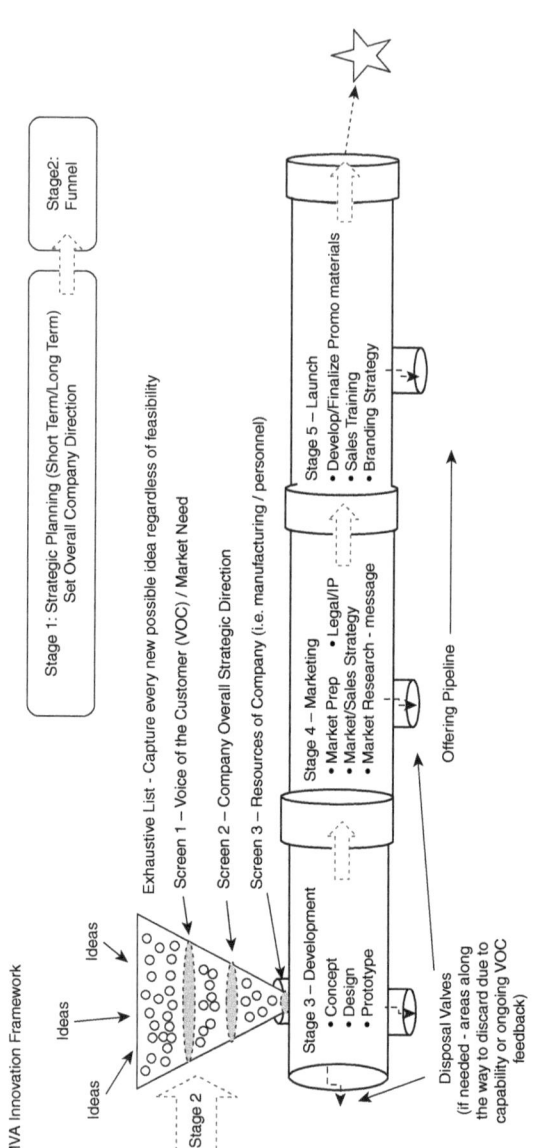

FIGURE 3.5 MVA Innovation Framework diagram
www.thefbcg.com

NEW PRODUCTS AND SERVICES   49

INNOVATION BY BUSINESS MODEL

An innovation need not be a new product or service. It can also represent a new *business model* or a different way to go to market. Michael Dell, for example, gave consumers the ability to create a made-to-order computer online, shrinking lead times and bypassing retail outlets to drive large profits.

In the family business domain, Uline grew from under $20 million in sales to over $2 billion in one generation—all by selling corrugated products and other packaging material! How did they do it? They created an evolutionary business model for the sector, based on quick delivery supported by a state-of-the art inventory system and fanatical attention to details. Their innovative approach turned brown cardboard into green money.

BEWARE THESE PITFALLS

While innovation can create much excitement and increased value in a family business, there are some issues of which to be mindful when looking to develop new products and services.

- **No Process**—It might seem obvious by now, but family firms that use a formal or semiformal process for innovation, such as those described here, are more likely to succeed with innovation. Those that don't, will likely struggle.
- **Imprisoned by the Past**—Family firms may feel overly burdened by their legacy of products or processes, which can impede them from thinking in a more visionary way about new offerings. Creating a healthy culture of innovation, as discussed in chapter 2 on the "Culture of Innovation," can combat this issue.
- **Family-free Innovation**—While innovation processes don't require a family member as a leader or champion, they are much more likely to proceed effectively with family members in key roles.
- **Too Many Pet Ideas**—Families run the risk of being overly tolerant of developing the pet ideas of family members in the business, which can

preclude the strongest ideas from prevailing. Members need to be able to "shoot their own dogs," as it's known in the field of innovation.

THINGS TO REMEMBER

- Product and service innovation is the largest area of family business innovation; such innovation, including in the context of new ventures, receives the largest proportion of resources in family businesses versus other activities.
- Drivers of product/service innovation in family business include personal attachments (such as customer and supplier relationships), controlled risk-taking, incremental development, low leverage, and a longer-term horizon.
- Innovative ideas are less effective without a disciplined process for bringing them to life. Formal innovation models include
  - the Stage-Gate New Product Process, which emphasizes achievement of specific milestones;
  - WinOvations, an extension of Planned Innovation, which involves the integration of people, coaching, and process;
  - Design Thinking, which emphasizes rapid prototyping at the intersection of human, business, and technical spheres;
  - the A-to-F Method, which specifies key roles that maximize innovation.
- Many successful innovative firms have followed a version of the MVA Innovation Framework, with specific stages from planning to launch.
- Families may also innovate by modifying their business model dramatically to address sector needs.
- Pitfalls related to product and service innovation include the failure to adopt an innovation process or to include family members in key innovation roles.

Chapter 4

Money and Metrics: Funding and Measuring Innovation

In 2007, when the Hartford school district decided to purchase its third-grade workbook from a competitor, the Grounder family executives at Ed-Zone knew it was time to get serious about developing more innovative products. Ed-Zone, a third-generation family business, had been a longtime leader in the educational tool space, based on its strong customer relationships and image as a cutting-edge player that adapted products quickly based on market needs. But that image had faded with the rise of digital technologies in the new millennium, including the digital teacher's companion book that Ed-Zone's competitor had offered the Hartford school system to help win their business.

Based on this and other developments, third-generation family members and Ed-Zone managers, Maria, Thomas, and Christine, sought to expand the business by creating more digital-friendly products for young students, entering new markets such as homeschooling, and experimenting with channels like online direct sales. The family knew progress would depend on creating a stronger culture of innovation, and their commitment to this had intensified after an outside board member detailed how her health food company had created an internal innovation center that had enabled the rapid development and launch of new products.

There was company-wide interest in boosting innovation to enhance the company's long-term prosperity. At the most recent board meeting, the Ed-Zone execs and family shareholders who served on the board voted to allocate more funds toward innovation activities. However, they also recognized the need for more clearly defined initiatives, resources, and metrics, and planned to have an in-depth discussion of these at the next board meeting. To gain innovation-related insights, two family members and three executives attended a Product Development and Management Association (PDMA) conference on innovation systems soon after the meeting. Similarly, a cross-functional team was sent to a workshop to refresh and expand the company's continuous improvement process, a system that had helped increase textbook quality and reduce development time significantly in past years.

Each third-generation family employee had his or her own take on the innovation challenge. Maria Grounder-Willis, VP of marketing and distribution, was a strong supporter of the push and knew it aligned with the spirit her grandfather and father had embraced while building Ed-Zone into a leading supplier of elementary education tools. She understood that the business had coasted on a long-lasting, popular series of workbooks and flashcards created in the 1980s that had quickly become a mainstay at many schools. Ed-Zone regularly modified the series based on market feedback, for example, adding multiple-choice quizzes to the workbooks when the Indianapolis school district asked for a fast way to test students' subject mastery. But most such improvements represented one-off enhancements, rather than new products for the market.

Ed-Zone's president, Thomas Grounder, who was Maria's brother, was well aware of this trend. "Why can't we develop a new set of flash cards for each school year?" he'd asked frequently, advocating a more disciplined innovation process. While the third generation appreciated the need to remain competitive, they remained *unsure how best to fund innovation and track its progress and results.* For example, as the bills arrived for the two recent innovation-focused initiatives (conference and workshop) and productivity dropped a bit as employees focused on continuous improvement, management recognized how easy it would be to spend money on initiatives in this area without a clear expected return. The Grounders needed a more strategic way to approach innovation and to measure its cost and results—new territory for them.

Christine Grounder, the youngest third-generation member working in the business, represented the family's hopes for a more innovative culture and process for developing and producing new offerings. After college she had worked in production for a California-based educational publisher for several years before earning her MBA at Tulane. Now working as a product manager for Ed-Zone, Christine was eager to apply her experience with metrics-driven production to the family business, and had recently begun sharing her ideas with her siblings and other executives.

* * *

Like many family enterprises, Ed-Zone sought to make innovation more central to its business model. Yet to maximize the value of change in any business, there must be mechanisms to fund it and measure its returns. The challenge is that innovation rarely comes neatly packaged; rather, it extends across product, divisional, and cost category boundaries, making it difficult to allocate funds and measure results without complexity and bureaucracy. So it's no surprise many family firms avoid developing funding and measuring systems for these initiatives.

FUNDING INNOVATION

Funding innovation strategically can be a complex challenge, but one that is worth undertaking for family enterprises.

Allocation Challenges

Unlike items such as payroll or insurance premiums, funding innovation activities and supporting a culture of innovation can't be reduced to one line on a family business's budget. Innovation can include items related to the R&D department, along with selective training courses, new market development, and even pricing strategy shifts. Moreover, innovation may represent only *part* of these activities, so it's important not to combine related funds with other expenses. Unfortunately, many firms routinely include noninnovative items, such as new tooling to stamp out commodity products, in their R&D budget, using it as a catch-all category. Thus, one challenge related to funding innovation is understanding what efforts and costs are actually considered innovation related in your family business.

Where to Find Innovation Funding

Because family firms like Ed-Zone tend to avoid heavy debt, they usually draw funding for innovation from *profits* rather than loans. That means balancing the firm's financial needs as related to strategic change with the other categories requiring cash. Here are the main categories to which profits from the family business are typically allocated:

- reinvestments in the business (including labor, equipment, potential acquisitions and various other capital needs)
- bonus/incentive programs
- distributions

Reinvestment in the business is the largest profit allocation category, and the one that would include funding earmarked for innovation. According to a recent FBCG survey, most family firms plow anywhere from 50 percent to 80 percent of profits back into the business.[1] For a first-generation, early-stage business that figure may well be 100 percent, if there are any profits at all. Once a family business develops an ongoing stream of revenue and profits, many firms begin to share the latter with employees through incentive programs and eventually with family shareholders through distributions or dividends. FBCG has found that about 15 percent of family business profits, on average, goes toward employee incentives (with a range from 5% to 25%), and anywhere from 2 percent to 20 percent of profits goes to shareholders, ideally based on the needs of the business and the expectations of family shareholders.

So, if a family firm wishes to increase its reinvestment funds that are allocated for innovation, it may consider reducing the amount going to employee incentives. This is tricky because incentives are a key driver of talent retention. A creative approach used by some family firms, then, is to invite a select group of nonfamily leaders to participate in a long-term incentive program. Such programs encourage a longer-term perspective among employees and foster the development of new opportunities and ideas—including those related to innovation—that may not show a return for several years.

Innovation funds are more likely to come from a reduction in shareholder distributions than a decrease in employee incentives. If the majority of shareholders is working in the business, they are more likely to accept lower distributions, as the business's long-term health is related directly to their livelihoods. If fewer shareholders are working in the business, there will typically be more resistance to reducing distributions. Shareholders who have grown accustomed to receiving distributions of a certain size don't give up these funds easily, even if they know that might be best for the business in the longer term.

Regardless of how firms secure funds for innovation, these must be allocated carefully, along with other money in the reinvestment category. Some businesses designate a percentage of their total budget to be allocated for activities that may include R&D, continuous improvement, outside consultants, training, patent application, and association membership. Some family firms belong to the Product Development and Management Association (PDMA), a nonprofit professional society that organizes and publishes information about the development of new products. In general, a proactive, multipronged approach to funding innovation contributes to a more pervasive culture of innovation.

In reality, many firms are forced to budget away any available funds before even considering future-oriented activities such as innovation. Highly predictable line items that tend to come before innovation include salary increases, computer- and technology-related costs, insurance, facility cleaning, and many more. Thus the process of budgeting for innovation often requires significant innovation itself.

How They Did It

Let's consider two family business examples of funding innovation: one positive, one not so positive. The Grounder family behind Ed-Zone decided to fund innovation in two ways. First, they agreed to cut shareholder distributions in half for two years while they developed a completely new line of digital workbooks and flashcards. External pressures, including customer expectations and competition, motivated the Grounders to be more decisive around this issue and to invest more significantly in innovation. Second, they budgeted about 5 percent of total operating expenses for two years to fund innovation, which included more aggressive continuous improvement activities, specifically the enhancement of their packaging and shipping process for software and electronic learning tools. The Grounders set 5 percent as a guideline rather than a firm target because they recognized innovation-related needs would likely change year to year. Moreover, to show the potential longer-term value of their new innovation funding, the family created a ten-year pro forma financial statement reflecting that a two-year decline in profits would be followed by increased returns over the next eight years. They also agreed that if they met the projected profit targets, they would reinstate the full distribution.

Contrast the example above to that of the Friar family, which owned multiple small U.S. newspapers. The Friars enjoyed a 30-plus year run of profitable publishing before the rise of digital media cut deeply into their returns. Family leaders recognized the business had to change quickly by investing in new technology, more digital-savvy talent, and facility consolidation. The challenge was that for decades the business had provided two generations with regular "fixed" distribution checks representing about 25 percent of annual profits, with the remainder going to essential new equipment and programs, facility maintenance, and acquisitions. As profits shrunk, dividends remained at the same dollar level, rising in proportion to represent over *half* of total profits. Because many family shareholders had adopted lifestyles that required regular, sizable distributions, there were no available funds for reinvestment in the business's future. Not surprisingly, the Friars had to close several lines of business, dramatically reduce dividends, and consider the sale of remaining assets to outside investors.

Funding Innovative Diversification

The core business is often considered the family's golden goose, representing as much as 90 percent of the family's cumulative wealth.[2] Those family firms that have generated sufficient wealth in the golden goose often desire to diversify outside their core offerings. Many put aside money for noncore business investments, to "reinnovate" the family enterprise into a healthier mix of businesses less dependent on single markets.

For example, the Hearst family, a very different media family from the Friars mentioned above, diversified outside its core newspaper businesses for much of its history. One high-return investment has been in ESPN, the

US sports television channel. The Hearst Corporation saw growing consumer demand for sports-related entertainment and believed sports content cost less to produce than other types of television offerings such as scripted shows. Hearst also partnered with Disney, ESPN's majority owner, to maximize its investment in this new area for the business. ESPN has continued to be one of the Hearst Corporation's most profitable holdings, demonstrating how visionary firms fund innovative diversification to boost continuity.

Sligh, a family-owned US furnishings company, was looking to diversify into a new furniture line to address growing demand for products that aid family communication. Instead of funding the entire project themselves, the family recruited a complementary mix of partner companies to share in funding and development for a royalty or unit fee. The outside furniture designer created a family communication center that included electronic charging stations for computers, phones, and other devices, along with a small whiteboard and postal mail holder. Sligh provided the brand name and marketing support, and the manufacturer underwrote prototype development in China. Along with funding-related innovation, the product represented strong elements of shipping innovation (the three modules involved could be nested together for more efficient transport) and low-cost production.

MEASURING INNOVATION

What gets measured gets improved. This adage applies to innovation, with the caveat that innovation is a difficult business area to measure, as suggested earlier. While CEOs participating in a Conference Board annual survey regularly cite innovation as one of their top challenges for long-term sustainability,[3] many express frustration with gauging their progress on this topic. Part of the measurement challenge is the wide range of definitions for what constitutes innovation-related performance results. Even the definition used in this book—that innovation should produce "meaningful results"—is open for interpretation. And when a family firm views innovation more holistically to include new products, new processes, new channels, new businesses, and the firm's entire culture, it makes the measurement challenge even greater.

As a result, there tends to be a mix of innovation-related metrics ranging from broad to quite specific. According to McKinsey, the companies securing the highest returns from innovation do use metrics well.[4] Key measurements cited in the McKinsey study, in increasing order of specificity, are

- overall revenue growth (based on assumption that revenue growth is driven partially by innovation);
- customer satisfaction;
- percentage of sales from new products or services;
- R&D spending as a percentage of sales;
- number of new products and services introduced.

3M is credited with pioneering an innovation measure that includes the *number* of new products introduced in the past three years, coupled with the *sales* from those products compared to all other sales. Family businesses don't traditionally capture these measures, in part because many "innovations" in such settings are modifications of existing products and services versus whole new products or services. Broad surveys of customers and/or employees may help identify or create best practices for the measurement of innovation. Similarly, family firms can learn from public companies, which tend to be more metrics driven. Such firms often use the number of patents and patent applications as indicators of innovation. One challenge is that some family firms prefer to keep their innovations proprietary, rather than sharing details in the public domain (i.e., through patent information).

After a series of board meetings, the Grounder family from our earlier example concluded they would use a variety of innovation measures:

- track the 5 percent of the budget allocated to innovation to understand where it went and what kind of return it generated;
- measure short-term (annual) and long-term potential (3+ years) returns on innovation;
- code new products and modifications in order to measure these as a percentage of total sales;
- measure 3 dimensions of innovation: new and modified products, new customers, and expansion into new geographic regions.

With large family businesses ($1 billion or more in annual sales), measurement of innovation often focuses on the development of entire new businesses created by internal entrepreneurs, sometimes referred to as "intrapreneurs." For example, multisector giant Cargill has an Emerging Business Accelerator (EBA) that evaluated more than 450 opportunities between 2004 and 2008. The accelerator invested in 13 ideas during that period, of which two have graduated into ongoing businesses, two were sold, four were discontinued, and five remain in the EBA portfolio.[5] EBA businesses have produced hundreds of millions of dollars in new revenues for Cargill. Thus, one potential measure of innovation is the number of new businesses developed and the returns they have generated.

Finally, family firms might measure innovation by the proportion of time devoted to it within the organization. Time has become a precious commodity as we have become a more digitally driven, efficient business world and society. While it's true that we can get more done now, it's not that we have created more time—just more tasks with which to fill it. Innovative thinking calls for time, often "inefficient" time to think and develop new ideas. In fact, those with the most time—from kindergarteners to convicts—have been shown to be the most creative! That's exactly why 3M encourages its designers and engineers to spend up to 15 percent of their time outside of their main projects. Family firms, already willing to experiment, can take a cue from this example with regard to encouraging and measuring innovation.

BEWARE THESE PITFALLS

- **Innovation overexuberance**—Some firms become overly focused on innovation (seeing it as a silver bullet) and engage in uncontrolled spending in this area. Early in its second generation, Ed-Zone overextended its efforts on developing new products and modifications simultaneously. Two bank covenants were breached, and the founder and son had to pull back dramatically on development work to save the firm.

- **Distributions over reinvestment**—Some firms sacrifice innovation-focused investment to preserve distributions. Founders may inadvertently create this scenario by overemphasizing financial support of the next generation, including those not working in the business. Aim for a healthy balance.
- **Mismeasurement of innovation**—There is a wide spectrum of innovation measurement, with some firms taking too rigid an approach (such as expecting immediate results) and others not measuring the results of innovation at all. Again, a balanced approach is optimal.

THINGS TO REMEMBER

- Funding and measuring innovation are important in generating the highest return from innovative efforts in the family business.
- *Funding* innovation includes challenges related to where to find funds—potentially from reinvestment funds (profits), distributions, or incentive programs—and how best to allocate them within the business, including as related to R&D, outside consultants, patents, and association membership; innovative diversification requires investment in noncore business offerings, to avoid dependency on single markets.
- *Measuring* innovation is tricky, due in part to the challenge of defining innovation-related performance results; potential measurements include R&D spending as a percentage of sales and of the number of new products/services introduced; firms may also measure the proportion of time devoted to innovation within the organization.
- Innovation-related pitfalls include uncontrolled spending in this area and the sacrificing of innovation to preserve distribution levels for family members.

Chapter 5

The Next Generation: Reinnovating the Family Business

The pressure was sometimes unbearable: keeping the Robar family food business prosperous into the fourth generation was proving far more challenging than anyone had predicted. As the food industry became increasingly competitive and commoditized, operating profits for the family's 14 grocery stores across the mid-Atlantic states had dipped below 2 percent, with little relief in sight. The Robars' five restaurants fared only slightly better, with margins around 3.5 percent. The family and its employees watched as their limited profits disappeared quickly to pay for items like badly needed parking lot resurfacing, new shopping carts, and larger display cases. Forced to make such necessary investments, the family found it virtually impossible to find the funds to attract and retain talent, pursue new business opportunities, provide jobs for upcoming family members, and fulfill the family's vision of giving back to their communities. The pressure weighed especially heavily on the third and the rising fourth generations, in whose hands rested the enterprise's future.

The Robars' foray into the food business had begun over a century earlier, in 1901, when brothers Kenyon and Art Robar began selling butter and milk from a horse-drawn wagon. As demand grew, the brothers added more dairy products like cheese and, in 1920, opened their first "cash-and-carry" store. Starting in the early 1950s, the family's emphasis shifted to full-service grocery stores. While profitable, the distribution and retail businesses competed for resources, preventing either from becoming a market leader.

Currently, three third-generation family members led the three main Robar businesses, under the banner of Robar Family Enterprises. Adam was president of Robar's Fresh Market (grocery business); Georgia, Adam's sister, ran the distribution business; Bill, Adam's cousin, led the restaurant business. The firm's board included these business leaders, two third-generation family members who did not work in the business, and three outside advisors.

The board and executives struggled with how to make the current businesses more profitable and how to move into potentially more lucrative areas. Discussions tended to become emotional as family members prioritized the businesses to which they had closer ties, often reducing their objectivity. Bill, known for his persuasiveness, was adamant about creating a new line of restaurants, but his siblings and cousins remained unconvinced. "Bill's not always right, but he's always sure!" family members said half-jokingly. Cheryl, one of the third-generation family directors who did not work in the business, suggested conducting more research related to this investment decision.

All board members agreed that they should ask the fourth generation—six cousins in total—to take a more active role in identifying future opportunities. The fourth generation refined and built upon a list of opportunities the third generation had started, including

- launching a catering business,
- buying out a local butcher to control meat, poultry, and fish preparation for the grocery and distribution businesses,
- starting a new brand of restaurants to leverage further Robar's history and assets,
- establishing a real estate company to purchase select properties near the firm's restaurants and grocery stores,
- spinning off the fledging food service distribution business,
- acquiring a vineyard and developing a Robar's wine line.

Like their predecessors, the younger Robars felt obligated to reinnovate the family business. But there was still so much to do just to maintain the core businesses. "Preserve the core while building for the future" became the family's mantra. The fourth generation had their work cut out for them, but they were excited about taking an innovative approach.

* * *

The Robars and most other multigeneration business families have heard the saying and the statistics: "Shirtsleeves to shirtsleeves in three generations," and only about 12 percent of family businesses make it through the third generation, according to multiple studies and the experience of FBCG advisors. Those firms that manage to prosper longer term typically display significant change or "reinvention" in each generation. A review of FBCG clients shows that long-lasting family enterprises build on their core strengths, competitive advantages, and emerging opportunities, often by managing the paradox of *sticking to your knitting while broadening your offering* better than do others. That means they have to respect their historical foundation—past generations' values, work ethic, traditions, and innovations—while adapting to market shifts and giving voice to the younger folks involved in the system. Diversifying into new product/service offerings often generates richer career opportunities for the next generation, a key development as more family members seek positions within the enterprise. In this chapter we'll examine what it takes to reinvent continually, with the support of each new generation.

INNOVATION ACROSS GENERATIONS

Most family businesses came into being because they created a different, new, or innovative product or service. The Robar's dairy product distribution was fairly innovative in the early 1900s. Each subsequent generation puts their imprint on the business, some more innovative than others. In the Robar's case,

- founders Kenyon and Art Robar delivered dairy products by horse, then modified an automobile into a dairy delivery vehicle to increase capacity, range, and speed;
- the second generation moved into retail grocery stores, innovating ways to keep products fresher through controlled climate techniques, including refrigeration in delivery vehicles and retail sites;
- the third generation created restaurants that leveraged Robar's food distribution and retail knowledge and assets to develop new competencies in this fast-growing market;
- the fourth generation has suggested innovative ideas that included diversifying into the real estate and alcoholic beverage sectors.

Such traditions of innovation arise from multiple factors: innovation-focused culture and values, innovator role models, market pressures, educational opportunities (such as business school), and many others. Enduring family businesses continuously seek innovation in multiple areas, including: products, processes, services, business models, promotion, distribution, diversification, and governance. The rising generation, typically less burdened by day-to-day business challenges and inspired with fresh ideas from school and outside experiences, often takes responsibility for changing and innovating the family business to succeed in future generations. In the Robars' case, the third generation struggled to break away from the demands of and personal ties to the current business model, and looked to their successors for a fresh perspective.

The need for fresh, relevant new ideas is a key reason to prepare the next generation for succession long before it's a reality. Values, the bedrock of a family and their business, form the most important foundational element. Sharing values-related stories around the dinner table, while not what we typically consider "innovation," is a great way to start. And many families we know have ensured that next-generation members' first jobs with the firm promote humility and perspective. Cleaning bathrooms, sweeping floors, sorting recyclable materials, and other manual tasks instill a humble attitude regarding the business and an appreciation for the importance of every job and operation within it.

Even simple games can promote important business and innovation lessons. Thomas Elghanayan, a member of a New York-based family real estate firm, recalls how he and his brother learned key business skills through hard fought, daylong Monopoly games. "Monopoly teaches you many long-term lessons: to buy property and build quickly," he told a *New York Times* reporter. "You can get wiped out by the randomness of the dice, or the vagaries of the market."[1] Such learning can form the foundation of innovation across generations.

DEVELOPING NEXT-GENERATION FAMILY MEMBERS

It's important to give younger family members, those in their 20s and 30s, learning opportunities and a voice in the business, especially when it comes to innovation. But what are the best ways to do that? One creative way is for younger-generation family members to network with family members from other companies. For example, Loyola University's Next Generation Leadership Institute has been a leader in this area, helping groom a high-potential group of next-gen family leaders. Similarly, the Family Business Alliance of West Michigan has helped form over ten Next Gen Peer Groups. Each group brings together seven to nine next-gen family members from different businesses with one facilitator, who is an experienced family or nonfamily executive.

The Next Gen Peer Groups are modeled after the highly successful Young Presidents Organization (YPO) Forum structure, which includes

- open, honest sharing of family and business issues,
- disciplined meeting format, including issue presentations,
- deep-dive topic discussions,
- strict confidentiality, and
- expectation of 100 percent attendance.

The Family Business Alliance hypothesized that shared experiences and knowledge would help members become stronger contributors to their family businesses. Using the YPO template as a guide, the alliance ran three pilot Next Gen Peer groups. Word got around, and many more groups were added quickly.

The peer group format has struck a meaningful chord for younger-gen family members, who represent a demographic that clearly values social networking in both face-to-face and virtual forms. These family members blossom as they share insights among themselves. Interestingly, the proliferation of digital networking has increased the need for more personal networking. Ellie Frey, director of the Family Business Alliance, recently said, "The Next Gen Peer Groups have turned out to be a very valuable service and like a hypergrowth business where our largest challenge is capacity—finding and training enough qualified facilitators!" Community leaders view the Next Gen Peer Groups as an important component of economic development, as ensuring that a capable younger generation is fundamental to enhancing family businesses' future contributions to regional and national economies. As such, peer-to-peer learning and support in family business are growing globally.

ENTERING, WORKING, EXITING

Much family business literature focuses on preparing a family member to enter the family business. Today, it is very common for firms to expect new entrants to have a college education and two to five years of professional experience outside the family business. Innovative family businesses now also include policies or guidelines for *working* in the business and *exiting* it.

Once a family member enters the business, the work has just begun. To develop into a strong contributor with leadership potential, including as it relates to innovation, takes careful planning and exposure to numerous elements of the business. In this regard, internal and external mentors and coaches have proven to be a valuable tool. An external mentor in particular can assist the younger family member in looking at the business from different perspectives and help drive change. New board members often fit this role well.

With regard to exiting the business, it's critical to have constructive departure processes—for the good of individual family members and the broader firm. One Minnesota-based family firm uses a sabbatical process, allowing members to leave for up to two years with some compensation as long as they are seeking new interests that could be of future value to the business. In one case, a 42-year-old second-generation executive embarked on a "leadership self-study" break. He read, studied, and "internalized" how he could apply the insights of renowned leadership thinkers, from Peter Drucker to Patrick Lencioni, to his leadership style. When he returned from his one-year sabbatical, his enhanced leadership skills and perspective were clear to everyone in the business. Fast-forward ten years to today: the family member is now president of the family business, and credits his time away with helping him build key skills for success.

Those next-generation members who choose not to work in the business may still show support as shareholders or potential shareholders, current or future board members, or family council leaders, or in other roles. Specific ways to contribute include

- sharing expertise,
- focusing on long-term strategy and policy,
- innovating
- ensuring organizational, group, or individual accountability,
- evaluating performance,
- participating in key strategic decisions,
- challenging givens *and* support decisions,
- networking,
- providing guidance through risk and reward evaluations,

- helping with succession or exit,
- ensuring compliance with government and industry regulations and standards, and
- providing a sounding board to those in leadership roles.

THE FAMILY OFFICE AND THE YOUNGER GENERATION

Those families who have created a family office as a result of a liquidity event or the generation of significant wealth from their operating business are in a cash-rich position with many investment decisions to make. Such fortunate family firms often try to diversify by innovating whole new ventures outside their main business, channeling related investments through a family office or family fund. These undertakings may be viewed as a way to educate and energize the younger generation by recruiting them to be involved in analyzing and recommending opportunities, especially innovative ones.

In his late 20s, Rick DeVos, grandson of Amway cofounder Rich DeVos, asked to launch several new business ventures outside the scope of the current family business. His parents wished to encourage their son's entrepreneurial spirit but also to ground him in business reality. Rick faced a high bar set by previous generations: Dick, his father, had led Amway into the international arena, which today accounts for the majority of the firm's business; Rick's mother, Betsy, comes from the enterprising family behind a specialty manufacturer of innovative products for automobile interiors. To harness Rick's creative energy, the family provided a "loose leash," seed money, and judicious advice to help the third-generation member create a host of ventures, including an Internet film business, an entrepreneurial award business, and an open art contest. The last, the highly acclaimed ArtPrize (www.artprize.org), has taken the art world by storm, creating an innovative way to engage an entire community in the conversation about art, while providing a great forum for artists to share their work.

SELECTING AND NURTURING INNOVATION RAINMAKERS

As shared in chapter 3, Greg Stevens of WinOvations carried out a study showing that people who place in both the Intuitive and Thinking categories of the Meyers Briggs Type Indicator personality test tend to be much stronger at innovation.[2] Identifying family members with this potent combination of creative analytics, or any other innovation-enhancing traits, can help infuse the firm with an innovative spirit as it relates to developing creative commercial products, shop floor processes, organization structures, office improvements, and so forth. But they will likely need training and support to discern which one or two of their many ideas have real commercial potential. Similarly, because most future family business leaders tend to be stronger in one area than the other, additional training in the less dominant area can be quite valuable. Such guidance takes thoughtfulness and persistence.

A family business making high-end office furniture decided to expand its product offerings aggressively. Leadership assigned a young fourth-generation member as head of the new business development process. Rising to the task, this leader has created a robust screening process to help determine which ideas will have the most positive impact. A key component of the process is to aim for a balance of opportunities that shifts the business from its high dependence on office furniture. The third-generation chairman and other family leaders are solidly behind the next-gen leader and his peers who will shape the business's future.

Third-generation business leader Keisuke Takemura of AS Corporation in Osaka, Japan, offers another example. Takemura found an innovative niche in the staid undergarment market, developing a hip line of underwear as a point of diversification for his family business. The Japan-based undergarment line has grown thirtyfold over the past five years!

Other family firms seek to match opportunities with projected future trends, another great area of opportunity for the younger generation. Mr. McGuire's advice ("Plastics") to Dustin Hoffman's character in the film *The Graduate* proved prophetic as the material took off in ensuing decades. Today, composite man-made materials continue to provide opportunities for growth and innovation. A third-generation family business with which we have worked has banked on this trend, using their core competencies to shift focus from manufacturing fiberglass boat hulls (the boat business declined over 50% in one year) to making composite-based wind turbine propellers, mass transit vehicle coatings, and other innovative products. Again, next-generation members have played a pivotal role.

Other emerging innovation forms and tools, such as *open innovation*, are often best led by the younger generation. The idea behind open innovation is that, in a world of widely distributed knowledge, companies cannot afford to rely entirely on their own research, but should instead buy or license processes or inventions (i.e., patents) from other companies. In addition, internal inventions that are not being used in a firm's business should be taken outside the company through licensing, joint ventures, or spin-offs.[3] For family businesses, it is more difficult to collaborate with outsiders, as there is always great fear of losing control or disclosing the "secret sauce" that makes the family business unique. Using the younger generation to push this particular innovation envelope while the senior generation acts as a governor can bring balance to this approach.

BEWARE THESE PITFALLS

- **Not Letting Go**—If the senior generation does not relinquish its leadership role, the next generation's impact will diminish. FBCG advisors find while age is not the sole indicator of when to let go, most effective transitions start when the senior generation is in its 50s and 60s. Once past 70 years old, if a patriarch or matriarch has not let go, it is likely he or she won't until the end.
- **Loose or Tight Leashes**—If the upcoming generation is given too much leeway in decision-making and reinnovating the

business, the level of risk can quickly go past the family's comfort zone as investments mount unchecked. On the other hand, giving the next generation too little latitude can sap innovation and encourage them to enter a play-it-safe mode that fails to promote healthy innovation.
- **Trapped by the Present**—An unwillingness to let the younger generation experiment and make mistakes leads to a culture of preserving the status quo rather than one emphasizing energetic development.

THINGS TO REMEMBER

- Reinnovation of the family business, especially as led by the upcoming generation, is critical.
- Traditions of innovation can be promoted by the sharing of values, role models within the organization, and educational opportunities (such as business school)
- Next-generation peer groups are particularly helpful for sharing innovation-related insights among rising family leaders.
- Internal and external mentors are also important sources of encouragement and guidance concerning innovation.
- The family office can be a valuable forum for allowing next-generation members to assess and recommend investment opportunities.
- People with a blend of creative and analytical skills tend to be effective innovators; identifying them within the organization and building such skills among multiple leaders help support innovation and reinnovation; rising-generation leaders are particularly skilled at identifying innovative diversification opportunities.
- Pitfalls related to reinnovation include the failure of the outgoing generation to cede power to their successors or to give them too much innovation-related leeway.

Chapter 6

Leadership and Ownership Transitions: Ensuring Succession Supports Innovation

In 2012, all three generations of the Brandon Family set sail on the Silver Seas Whisper, an upscale cruise ship traveling from Miami to the Grand Caymans and other Caribbean islands. Along with enjoying time together, the Brandons planned to conduct a series of family meetings to address a number of succession matters related to the highly successful business they owned: Dundee Enterprises, a multinational packaging supplier. Soon after departing Miami, Louise, Jacob, Charles, and Laura—all second-generation Brandon siblings in their late forties and early fifties—huddled around a deck table remembering their father, Henry, who had passed away the previous year, prompting urgent succession-related questions related to both ownership and leadership.

"You know how Dad disliked the idea of a major inheritance," Louise reminded her siblings. They recalled one of Henry's favorite quotes: "Monetary gifts weaken one's work ethic." The Brandon patriarch was passionate about continuing the business and wanted his children to work hard to do so. Jacob, his eldest child, agreed. He felt it was their generation's responsibility to continue building the family's wealth and pass on the majority of their assets to the upcoming generation, providing his three children and their cousins a solid base of business value to build upon. All the siblings agreed with their father's notion that private enterprises, particularly family businesses, do a great job investing funds, deploying resources, and creating meaningful employment opportunities. They saw any succession decisions driven by the related themes of family business continuity and societal contribution.

As far as specific succession-related measures, the family had already worked diligently with their estate attorney and tax accountant to minimize estate tax issues and efficiently transfer wealth between generations. They had established various trusts and a shareholder agreement, yet these documents did not fully resolve multiple complex issues related to the family's assets or the leadership of their company. One ongoing debate concerned what proportion of annual profits should go toward family members' distributions versus the family foundation, which served multiple important causes. Such issues figured into succession decisions for both ownership and leadership.

Dundee Enterprise had grown dramatically over just two generations, from a $20 million distributor of office supplies soon after its founding to a billion-dollar global packaging material supplier. The growth had helped attract family members to join the company, and Dundee currently employed four second-generation members and five from the third generation. However, as the business grew in size and complexity, it required significantly more advanced leadership skills. In reality, few currently employed people—family or nonfamily executives—possessed the talent necessary to lead a 4,000-employee company with 12 operation/distribution sites.

Leadership had become an even more urgent concern when Henry suddenly passed away from a heart attack, with only a vague verbal succession plan in place. He had put off the decision to select the next president and had failed to build sufficient executive bench strength to match the business's growing complexity. Jacob, Henry's eldest child and the most experienced in the business, was thrust into the president role upon Henry's passing, leaving open his critical position as senior vice president of distribution. Still, many leadership holes remained unfilled, requiring thoughtful solutions.

On the ownership side, over 80 percent of the Brandon family's total wealth was concentrated in Dundee Enterprises, of which they were sole owners. The other 20 percent of the family's wealth was tied to real estate and other investments. There had been past liquidity events, and the family had received a major distribution from a bank agreement recapitalization five years earlier. The business's estimated value had tripled since then and, while another recapitalization was possible, the family's growing wealth made it increasingly difficult to pass ownership to the next generation while maintaining the Brandons' historical values. Teaching financial literacy and responsible stewardship to the youngest family members was crucial, and the family had arranged for an expert on finance to facilitate a session for young family members during the cruise.

Literally and metaphorically, the Brandon family members were all in the same boat—tethered to a family firm that yielded wonderful returns, yet required innovative succession solutions for business continuity and maintenance of family values and harmony. They kept this in mind as they debated their plan for the future.

* * *

THE CHALLENGE OF SUCCESSION

One of the most challenging dimensions of family business, and one that can benefit greatly from innovative approaches, is succession. Ownership and leadership transitions are never as simple as "handing over the keys." The stakes are high. Even a family business with a great lineup of innovative products and services can join the large ranks of failed family enterprises if it doesn't have appropriate succession plans in place.

In other words, succession can be innovative in itself, but it also serves to support other elements of innovation within a family business. This may in fact be the greater value of the succession process. Successful transitions help keep the innovative spirit alive and/or reenergize a family business with regard to how to reevaluate product offerings, business models, channels of distribution, the overall culture, or other key areas.

Leadership is about guiding a business with regard to strategy, finance, operations, and other general management areas, while ownership is about controlling the firm's stocks and assets. Sometimes the two components of succession are accomplished simultaneously. In other cases, they occur at different times, in different business phases, with different people. In the case of a solo first-generation founder, the individual is almost always the natural owner and leader. If two siblings start a business, as was the case with Duration Ag Products (discussed in chapter 1), then ownership will depend on how the business was incorporated, and leadership will often be shared as the business is developed. Subsequent generations with multiple family members are faced with much more uncertain paths to ownership and leadership, because of the many factors involved. Leadership-related issues include the next generation's interest in and qualifications for working in the business, along with the outgoing generation's acceptance of any leadership transition. Ownership-related factors include deciding whether to keep the business family owned, determining financial security for the outgoing generation, addressing market conditions, and dealing with the next generation's interest in ownership. These factors typically evolve over years, resulting in varying degrees of complexity and conflict.

A FOUNDATION FOR SUCCESSION

Prior to considering innovative approaches to succession, let's examine three fundamental components that help create a solid foundation for any transitions (along with supporting innovation):

- family and business foundational beliefs—values, vision, mission
- strategic business planning
- organization and governance structure

First, having *family and business foundational beliefs* in place, as embodied in the firm's stated values, vision, and mission, helps family members develop effective criteria for leadership and ownership succession. A clearly stated value of Dundee Enterprises is meritocracy: the family values family members' demonstrated contribution, applied knowledge, and earned position. This value and others will guide their approach to selecting leaders. The family's mission statement also includes the idea of giving back to the community, so next-generation leaders and owners will be expected to adhere to this.

The second foundational element is *strategic business planning*. Even though there is a correlation between having a written business plan and long-term family business continuity, less than one third of family businesses create a written plan. A plan ensures greater understanding of what needs to be accomplished and what type of leader is needed to take the business to the next level.

Finally, having an *organization and governance structure* that includes family members in appropriate positions (as discussed in the next chapter) provides a strong infrastructure that facilitates succession and innovation.

LEADERSHIP SUCCESSION

A leadership succession provides a natural time to innovate and lay the groundwork to support ongoing innovation. Change is in the air, and the organization is more open to new ideas. Still, it's important for the family business to first express and understand its values regarding its ideal type of leader. Will a leader be chosen based on merit (business capability) or mostly because he or she is part of the family? The issue of "family first versus business first" is front and center in the selection of a family business leader. A family member often leads the business for its early generations, with the goal of meeting the needs of both the business and the family. Enduring firms typically move toward "business-first" decision-making, while still honoring their history and future as a family business. That is, merit becomes a stronger leadership criterion over time, as family businesses select the best leader from a pool that includes family members and nonfamily executives within or outside the company. FBCG experience suggests that family businesses lean toward this business-first approach, while providing family members with the "inside" position for selection.

Historically, the least innovative method for leadership succession has been simply selecting the first-born male as the successor. This *primogeniture* approach has centuries-old roots based on religious and other societal norms. Over time, society has recognized that factors other than first-born status should figure into succession. Moreover, not every family business has an eldest son available as a leader!

Today, there are a number of options for leadership succession. The most effective leadership succession process starts very early. Innovative family firms have created training and experiential programs that enable younger-generation members to learn the business and internalize the family's values. Over the past four decades, the majority of family firms has agreed on at least two key requirements for family members who are entering the business: (1) a college degree and (2) outside work experience for two to five years. These once-innovative requirements are now standard practice, and some firms have beefed them up. Bissell, Inc., maker of vacuum cleaners and related products, now requires family members who are working for the company to obtain an MBA from a Top 10 business school. Some families require business experience in a specific industry, typically one related to their own.

Next, we examine several approaches to leadership succession, including the innovative elements that some family enterprises apply to them. Remember: getting leadership succession right helps support ongoing innovation in your business by ensuring the presence of leaders with innovative mind-sets and signaling that the firm embraces change of any form, rather than resisting it.

Outgoing Generation Decides

The outgoing generation often selects successors. Outgoing-generation leaders generally have the most intimate knowledge of upcoming family leaders' experience and abilities. Challenges arise when there are too many qualified candidates, or too few. And, of course, the decision-making process and outcome can take years, sometimes decades, and cause great family angst.

John A. Mellowes, third-generation family leader of Wisconsin-based steel producer Charter Manufacturing Company, had to make a succession decision between his sons: Charles and John W. John A. had led the business for over 30 years, growing Charter from under $100 million in annual revenues to well over $1 billion, the most dramatic generational growth it had experienced. The third-generation leader had a knack for strategy and risk-taking, creating a high-growth business with a family-friendly culture. This was a tough act to follow.

John A. and his fellow family- and nonfamily executives recognized that the model of a single family leader was not ideal for Charter's next phase, given the business situation and the next generation's capabilities. As such, they advocated a *sibling team* approach to succession, including an appropriate role for each son. After much deliberation and guidance from his advisors, the patriarch decided that Charles would become chairman since he was more of a group-minded big-picture thinker, and John W. would become president and CEO because he had more experience with strategy and operations. By taking a creative approach to the leadership transfer, John A. leveraged each son's capabilities, while galvanizing the family, executive team, and board to support the new leadership structure. The succession has proven very effective, as evidenced in part by Charter's ongoing innovation of products and services.

When there are multiple outgoing leaders and candidates to replace them, the selection process becomes more complicated. At Dundee Enterprises, for example, the four current-generation siblings will have to consider successors from among many upcoming cousins. The Padnos Company, a scrap and recycling business, decided it was not beneficial nor worth the stress within the family to select among four family members, all of whom had strong academic backgrounds and deep experience in the business. So they formed an *Office of the President* where the third-generation leaders work together, dividing key responsibilities based on their complementary strengths. Given the overlap in leadership, this approach requires strong family relationships, clarity on responsibilities, and well-managed egos for success. The current family leaders realize that while this leadership model has worked for them, it is unlikely to be the model for the next generation because of greater age differences and other factors. It is common to see divergent succession and leadership approaches for each generation.

Independent Succession Task Force Decides

Instead of leaving the decision to a senior family member or group to select the next leader, many family firms have developed a leadership succession task force comprised of nonfamily advisors. Such a task force can take significant pressure off current family leaders by securing a succession recommendation from an objective outside body. According to family business advisor John L. Ward, "The task force serves as an independent entity under the authority of the board, which has ultimate responsibility for selection of leaders."[1] The succession task force's composition varies by situation. Sometimes it is an ad hoc board committee that includes the independent outside board members. The task force could also include the company's HR leader, a family business advisor, a nonmanagement family leader, and a senior executive who is not affected by the succession.

A task force can be innovative in its approach to leadership succession. One task force outlined four alternatives for a succession plan to determine a family firm's next president and CEO:

1. transitioning to a new family leader,
2. transitioning to a current nonfamily executive,
3. bringing in an outside executive,
4. developing a hybrid of the options above, such as a family leader working alongside a nonfamily leader,

As the task force continued to evaluate these four alternatives, a fifth alternative emerged:

5. changing the required retirement age to allow the current, highly effective family leader to continue

The task force recommended the innovative last option to the family board members, who agreed, while noting they likely wouldn't have accepted a similar suggestion from the family leader.

An independent task force that worked with the Oliver Products Company, a multigeneration family business mentioned earlier in the book that produces medical device packaging and specialty food-processing equipment, recommended a hybrid family/nonfamily approach. They suggested recruiting an experienced outside executive to run operations as president, while retaining an experienced family member as CEO and to serve as the face of the business to customers and suppliers, since the family business image was very important in their industry. An independent board member became the chairman. The blended leadership team guided the business successfully for well over a decade. In another example, automaker Ford took a similar approach when it recruited Boeing executive Alan Mullaly as CEO in 2006, based on the company's dramatic scale of growth and complexity—something with which Mulally had much more experience than did Ford family members. These strategic succession maneuvers ensure smooth leadership transition and the support of current and future innovation.

Executive Leadership Decides

Similar to the succession task force, family firms may use the executive leadership team to make succession decisions. This can work, provided the team does not include a member who is a candidate for the position. The approach is particularly appropriate when the age gap between the outgoing and the incoming generations is large enough to require an interim leader to bridge the gap. The patriarch of the family who owns Custer Workplace Interiors, a specialist in office interiors, had three sons. But as he neared retirement, his sons were at least ten years away from leadership roles, and it was unclear which one was best suited to lead the company. So the patriarch/CEO brought in a nonfamily interim leader who was tasked with observing the sons, while working closely with them. During that time Custer also leaned heavily on its advisory board members and nonfamily executives to help make the succession decision. The best interim nonfamily executives will have deep knowledge of the business and the family's culture and values, along with its approach to innovation, and also understand that their tenure as leader of the business is temporary and transitional.

Incoming Generation Decides

In one family business with whom we have worked, the father/founder wished to create a succession plan, but wasn't sure which of his children would make the best next leader. Moreover, he knew that if he chose one, the others might not accept the decision. Having always emphasized collaboration, the founder asked his children to work together to determine the best future roles for each of them in the business, including CEO. Half-jokingly, he asked them to make a decision that same day! While they couldn't achieve that, the siblings met regularly over several months and resolved the issue of roles to everyone's satisfaction, including their spouses. Entrusting the younger generation with succession-related decision-making led to greater performance and morale than a decision by the founder's fiat would have, and supported the idea of open-mindedness on this key dimension.

A Death in Salzburg: Preparing for Emergency Succession

Too many family businesses have no succession plan in place, innovative or otherwise. Sometimes they discover the hazards of this the hard way: when a family leader dies or becomes otherwise unable to lead. Henry Brandon of Dundee Enterprises hadn't prepared for succession before he died, sending the business and family into crisis mode. We have seen instances where the death of a family business leader means the death of the business. In contrast, businesses with a strong succession plan in place typically get through even such a difficult crisis.

Monarch Hydraulics, Inc., provides one of the best examples of preparation for a succession crisis. The leadership team, which included three brothers and a cousin of the fourth-generation of the Jackoboice family, held an off-site "crisis succession" exercise in the early 1990s. The daylong exercise was designed to develop key measures for strategy, financials, and operations in case the unexpected happened, and included a series of questions asked of individual leaders regarding their future potential absence. The questions ranged from personal ("What would you like your tombstone to read?") to practical ("How should we handle your business relationships if you're no longer here?"). The leaders captured the resulting conversations and guidelines in a short document titled "Crisis Succession" that detailed how to handle the loss of any one of them.

In 1999, George Jackoboice, Sr., the company's president and one of the three leaders who had conducted the exercise, died of a heart attack while visiting his daughter in Salzburg. While still in a state of shock and grief, the surviving leaders pulled out the document to guide them in the leadership decisions that they had thought through during their earlier "no pressure" session. By the following Monday morning, George's office had been rearranged to reflect his absence, a letter had been sent to employees, customers, and suppliers, and George's replacement had been selected—all of these measures were influenced by what the leaders learned from the innovative crisis succession exercise.

How the Brandons Did It

While on the Caribbean cruise, the Brandon family of Dundee Enterprises mapped out the career goals and aspirations of each family member who was working in the business, along with his or her current skills. They used this information to develop a preliminary training and development plan for each member. The process made apparent that Jacob was the best choice for family leader of the business, even though he did not yet possess his father's range of product knowledge. Moreover, motivated by the unexpected recent loss of the patriarch, the family laid out several measures to address what would happen if Jacob could suddenly not perform the role of president. In this way, the Brandons disembarked from the cruise with a roughed out, mutually agreeable leadership succession development plan and an emergency leadership plan, all of which could support innovation throughout the firm.

OWNERSHIP SUCCESSION

"It was easier and more fun creating wealth than it has been figuring out how to preserve, transfer, and give it away," said a second-generation member of a successful family business. She's not alone in feeling that way. Like leadership succession, passing on ownership from generation to generation is one of the most complex aspects of family business continuity. Ownership, or who owns how many and what type of shares, is a legal fact. Once an ownership decision has been made, it is usually difficult to change without large-scale agreement.

Even when some senior family leaders prefer to give money to the family foundation (like Henry Brandon, deceased patriarch of Dundee Enterprises, did), there is still significant value in the actual business that must be transferred. Stocks and assets need to go to someone. A family business can be sold, gifted, liquidated, or some combination of these. The vast majority of owners opt to transfer the business to other family members, most often through a combination of gifting and selling. Creative estate attorneys and tax accountants have devised an array of legal means to transfer ownership while minimizing tax liability. It's a form of family business innovation that has been around for a long time and, like leadership succession, an important way in which to support other innovation throughout the enterprise.

Two Historical Examples of Innovative Ownership Succession

Henry Ford is well known for his innovation of the manufacturing assembly line and the visionary practice of paying workers $5 per day in the early 1900s, enough to allow them to afford the product they were producing. But he also displayed innovation with regard to ownership. From 1919 to 1956, members of the Ford family, the Edison Institute, and the Ford Foundation owned all the company's stock. When the company went public in 1956, the family retained control of the business through the voting shares owned by the Ford Foundation. Even today, "descendants of the founder maintain effective control through Class B *supervoting* stock that gives them 40% of the common stock vote."[2] Although nonfamily shareholders have expressed occasional discontent with the Ford family's effective control, it is difficult to argue with the company's innovation-driven performance over the past decade, compared to the other two major US auto companies—General Motors and Chrysler—both of which went into bankruptcy before being turned around.

Publishing icon William Randolph Hearst was another family business pioneer who displayed innovation in both business and ownership. His estate plan effectively utilized living trusts to manage the business and protect his heirs. To ensure his heirs benefited from his business's wealth without transferring money to them outright, Hearst created a 13-member trustee board made up of five family members and eight Hearst Corporation executives.[3] The trust was tasked with helping manage the company and its vast holdings, along with making yearly distributions to Hearst's descendants. Despite being sued by multiple parties for three generations, the trust has survived and continues to serve its original purpose—although it will end when the last of Hearst's grandchildren passes away.

The Fords and the Hearsts represent two high-profile families who have created innovative ownership transition approaches. But you needn't be part of such a prominent family business to exercise innovation in this area, as the next section suggests.

Innovative Ownership Succession

The end of 2012 saw the United States' greatest transfer of wealth in history. The reason was no mystery: family business owners and other wealthy individuals weren't sure how legislation that was in process might change estate and gift tax exemptions and other rulings, and took preemptive steps in case the laws changed the "wrong" way. Estate planners and tax advisors busied themselves using well-established and creative means to move wealth between generations. It is notable that most other countries do not have estate taxes or the degree of taxable transfers as in the U.S.

During more normal periods, U.S. families have more time to craft ownership succession strategies. Some of the often-used innovative techniques that family businesses have found most beneficial include

- an irrevocable life insurance trust (ILIT),
- a grantor retained annuity trust (GRAT),
- an intentionally defective irrevocable trust (IDIT),
- a gift of interest in family limited partnership,
- a qualified personal residence trust (QPRT),
- a self-canceling installment note (SCIN),
- a charitable lead trust (CLT),
- a charitable remainder trust (CRT),
- a dynasty trust, and
- a generation-skipping trust (GST).

These techniques each require deeper explanations of their appropriate use. Accounting and legal advisors who practice estate planning are the go-to experts for applying any of these options.

Family businesses, under the guidance of their attorneys and accountants, have also created different classes of stock to maintain control of the company over generations. A common approach here is the use of B shares, or common and nonvoting shares, for the younger generation, while the senior generation retains voting shares that allow them to vote for board members and control other key strategic items outlined in a shareholders agreement or buy/sell agreement. A more sophisticated approach is the development of supervoting shares, like those Henry Ford created.

Another important ownership succession issue applies to the valuation of the business. In order to secure a low cost basis for tax reasons, the Internal Revenue Service (IRS) in the U.S. allows discounting opportunities in the form of minority interest, or lack of control and lack of marketability. In order to allow family members to exit the business, redemption policies are often tied to these valuations. Some families often find it better for family harmony to provide a higher stock value than the maximum discounted price allowed for lack of marketability and minority interest when a family shareholder is seeking stock redemption. However, for gifting purposes transferring stock at the lowest acceptable value is still considered the most tax-efficient way to move family business wealth to the next generation.

We should also consider some of the more off-the-beaten-path approaches to ownership succession:

- *Random allocation of ownership*—The Elghanayan family divided their $3 billion New York real estate empire by asking each member of the upcoming generation to randomly select an envelope containing specific properties.
- *Gifting to "unborn" children*—Younger, wealthy entrepreneurs who do not yet have children or even know whether they will create a family business can use a grantor retained annuity trust (GRAT) for the benefit of descendants not yet born. Facebook founder (and billionaire) Mark Zuckerburg, who does not yet have children, used this technique to place stock into a trust prior to the company's going public. Senior-generation family members who are hoping to become grandparents can do the same for unborn grandchildren.
- *An IPO for future philanthropy*—The Steelcase Corporation, controlled by three third-generation families, opted to take the business public in order to provide some liquidity for family members who wished to pursue philanthropy in their later years. The families still controlled over 75 percent of the stock after taking the firm public, thus ensuring maintenance of control.

Finally, some families have taken a broader perspective of ownership succession, one that goes beyond the financial. "It is better to transfer values than wealth," claims one business owner. While in reality there is usually wealth that must also be transferred, if money-related values are clear, then the transition can go much more smoothly. We have found that family businesses endure much longer when they focus on transferring both values and wealth, as opposed to only the latter. A few creative families have even developed "letters of wishes," or nonlegal stipulations, for how they'd like their assets to be transferred to and used by the next generation. While not legally binding, these can be emotionally powerful means of transfer that increase the odds of family continuity.

It's important to remember that ownership succession—whether reflecting innovation in itself or not—is an important way of supporting innovation across the firm. Taking a clear-eyed, systematic approach to transitioning ownership will serve as a strong foundation for innovation and other important processes.

BEWARE THESE PITFALLS

- **Late Start on Succession**—An effective succession journey typically takes years, not months. We have found that when sufficient planning for both leadership and ownership succession is not begun at least *five years* prior to transitioning, there is a good chance the transition will be difficult for the business and the family.
- **No Emergency Plan**—Families that have no emergency plan in place face great stress and complexity when faced with an unexpected need for succession. Thoughtful emergency planning is critical.
- **Groupthink**—It is easy for family members to be overly homogeneous in their thinking regarding succession and other areas. Injecting more diversity of thinking and opinion (through outside board members, for example) can lead to creative decision-making and, oftentimes, innovation that adds real value.

THINGS TO REMEMBER

- A healthy succession process for both leadership and ownership can support innovation throughout a family business while reflecting innovation in itself.
- A good foundation for any succession includes family and business foundational beliefs (values, vision, mission), strategic business planning, and strong organizational and governance structure.
- Leadership succession has evolved significantly from the primogeniture approach of naming the first-born male as successor. Current approaches include
    - selection by the outgoing generation,
    - selection by an independent task force,
    - selection by executive leadership,
    - selection by the incoming generation.
- Leadership succession is an especially important component of emergency planning.
- There is an array of means for transferring ownership of a family business, including multiple creative trusts, partnerships, notes, and even random allocation.
- Clarity on money-related values will enhance the smoothness of ownership succession
- Pitfalls related to succession include getting a late start, failing to plan for emergencies, and facilitating groupthink.

Chapter 7

Governance: Overseeing Key Relationships to Support Innovation

In 2010, as Bradley Carter prepared the agenda for Transom Security Systems' next quarterly board meeting, he thought hard about how to address several tricky issues. Transom, which provides commercial and residential security systems, had been started outside Atlanta, Georgia, by Theodore Transom in 1948. Originally a specialty lock producer, the company grew to offer customized security systems including web-based monitoring cameras and infrared ID/entry cards. Walter, Theodore's only son, took over the company in 1978 and built it into a premier southeastern US security player with 750 employees and over $200 million in sales. Walter's sisters, Lucille and Cheryl, worked in the business when they were younger, but since 1975 had served on the board as family shareholders, each with 10 percent ownership and substantial annual distributions.

Governance of Transom had become an urgent issue, especially since 76-year-old Walter had declined quickly after being diagnosed with Alzheimer's. Millie, Walter's wife, who had never worked in the business, and her two oldest children, George and Elizabeth, who held leadership roles within Transom, had understood that Walter wanted Bradley Carter, a longtime friend and Transom board member, to take over as board chair once Walter was no longer capable of serving in that role. The transition had come more quickly than expected, however, as Walter had confessed after the last board meeting that he couldn't remember what had been discussed and it was "time to retire."

Now, acting chair Bradley and four outside advisory board members originally picked by Walter—now in their 70s and 80s themselves—struggled to manage the company's leadership succession and governance. They hoped to integrate what they knew of Walter's wishes for the business with the ideas of younger-generation family members, in particular George and Elizabeth. In addition, Bradley, chair of his own family business (about half the size of Transom), and Walter had previously discussed the need to formalize Transom's board and transition it to a fiduciary board, but hadn't felt the urgency to do so since the advisory board had functioned well for over a decade. Now Bradley wondered if it was time to approach the transition.

Bradley and Transom's other advisors had to take into account the expectations of multiple executives, family members, and outside partners. For example, Fred Mcalley, president of Transom, had been with the family business for 28 years. Ten years ago, Walter had allowed Fred to purchase 5 percent of the shares of Transom at a 50 percent discount, in part to ensure Fred's long-term tenure with the firm, especially during the generational transition. The stock carried no voting rights, yet Fred was a proud owner who participated in all advisory board meetings, typically guiding these meetings after Walter called them to order. Fred assumed he would work in a similar fashion with Bradley.

George and Elizabeth also worked in the business. George, 44, reported to Fred as vice president of operations; Elizabeth, the 39-year-old head of marketing, also reported to Fred. Valerie and Jeff, the third-generation siblings of George and Elizabeth, did not work in the business, although Jeff held a 5 percent ownership share. Valerie chaired the family council, which had been started three years ago to provide more structured education opportunities for the younger generation and to serve as a forum for sharing business-related information with the extended family. As the board meeting approached, Valerie was trying to complete several action items from the education committee so that a speaker on philanthropy would be well armed to present to the family at an upcoming session. In addition to trying to complete this task, Valerie and fellow council members were frustrated that many family members could not attend the session (a common problem), and wondered how to increase involvement. One other third-generation family member—Lucille's son, Bill—worked at Transom as a security system programmer and installer, and Valerie's husband, Ron (a third-generation spouse), was an accountant with the business. Transom's actual legal board of directors comprised only family members: Walter, Millie, George, Elizabeth, Lucille, Cheryl, and Jeff.

The four third-generation siblings and their cousin, Bill, had 25 children among them; fourth-generation members ranged in age from 2 to 31. Bill's daughter Alicia had recently joined the company in a production-planning position after working five years at an outside family business. Alicia was actively lobbying HR for a higher salary, when Bradley and Fred thought the incoming compensation package had already been finalized. Thus family member compensation became an important board agenda topic.

During a severe market downturn, a local investor with a successful real estate development company had provided $2 million to support Transom's LLC, which owned the business's new headquarters, in exchange for a 30 percent stake in that LLC. Since the real estate LLC had similar family ownership participation as the parent business, and the main operating business was tied to a long-term lease agreement, property ownership was a frequent topic at board meetings. Thus, alongside the central issue of leadership succession and other matters mentioned above, Bradley added property ownership to the agenda since the cash flow from the building could affect the family's financial situation.

* * *

The Transom Security example reflects a number of important questions related to family business governance, including

- what type of board is most effective for the business—advisory or fiduciary?
- who should be on the board?
- how do leadership and ownership succession affect governance?
- what impact does an outside investor have on governance?

- how should board meetings be conducted?
- should nonfamily members own stock?
- how do family members who are not working in the business gain a voice in the business?
- who should determine what policies should be in place for family employment?

While the Transom family had governance policies and guidelines in place already, to address the questions above and others effectively, and ensure business and family continuity, they needed to take a thoughtful, innovative approach to governance. Like the leadership and ownership succession processes discussed in the last chapter, governance can reflect an innovative approach in family firms, including as related to the roles family and nonfamily members take in the broad enterprise. But its greater value, often, is in supporting an innovative culture and meaningful ongoing change across dimensions.

Broadly, getting governance right means optimizing relationships among *family members, shareholders*, and *managers* such that the enterprise and each constituent group prosper.[1] Moreover, there are three key entities that have the most influence on family business governance: the board of directors, the family council, and the executive team, as depicted in Figure 7.1.

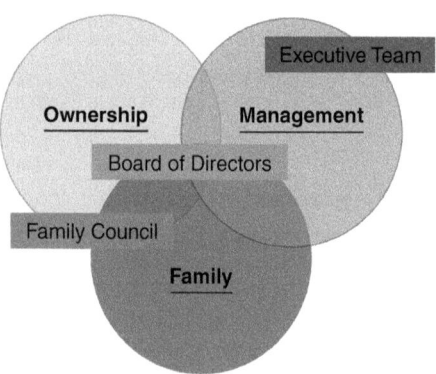

FIGURE 7.1 The 3-Circle model: the board of directors, the family council, and the executive team

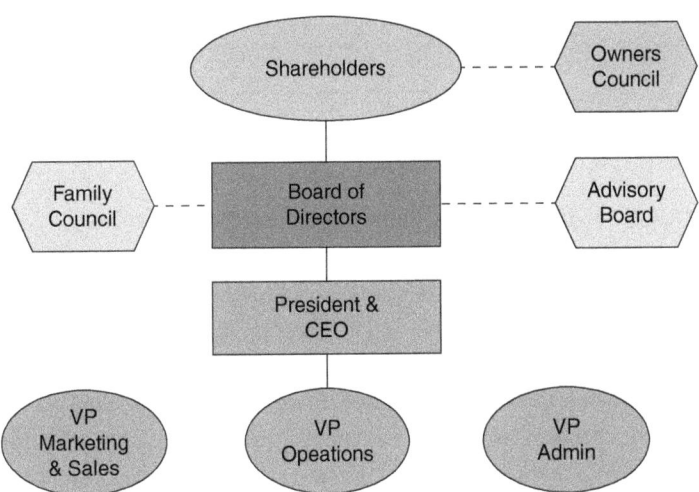

FIGURE 7.2 Simplified Governance Structure

Building on the 3-Circle model and its relationship to governance, figure 7.2 presents a simplified structure for how the governance entities above may be related in a family enterprise. Note that solid lines symbolize decision-making authority, whereas dotted lines depict influence, rather than formal authority. The next sections consider each of the governance bodies in more detail, followed by a discussion of where individual family members fit into the enterprise's overall structure, with the understanding that making strategic, sometimes innovative, governance decisions will support change across the firm.

BOARD OF DIRECTORS

An active board of directors, either advisory or fiduciary, including *independent outside* directors—experienced business persons who are not family members, executives in the business, or fee-based advisors (such as attorneys)—sets the optimal governance oversight tone in a family business. FBCG studies have shown that the highest-performing family firms tend to

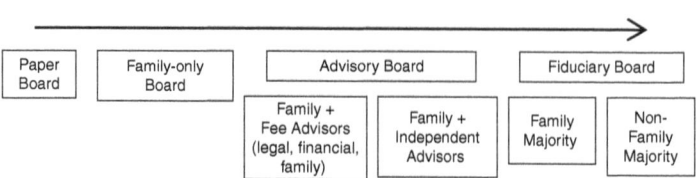

FIGURE 7.3 Evolution of Family Business Board Forms

have a fiduciary board with the majority of board members as independent outsiders versus family members.[2] The question, then, is how best to create such a board. The boards of most family businesses that get it right have *evolved* into an ideal form, rather than starting as one. That is, they transition from a "paper" board—described as one that exists only on paper, including annual minutes and required legal documents—to a family-only board, to an advisory board, to a fiduciary board with family members as the majority, to a fiduciary board with nonfamily members as the majority (see figure 7.3). This evolution nicely reflects incremental innovation, in that each stage represents a meaningful change from the previous one.

As with incremental innovation in product development, family businesses that evolve their board structures to meet the growing needs of the family and the business gain greater understanding and appreciation for the complexities of the governance process, as well as for how best to harness the board with regard to innovation and other key areas. Transom, for example, was considering whether to evolve its advisory board into a more formal fiduciary board—a move that would require some adjustment, but likely pay off over time. Beyond the board's form, several other dimensions are important to consider, as discussed below.

Size and Composition

An FBCG survey of 360 family business boards shows the average size to be six board members, with five to nine as optimal.[3] While data suggest that boards with a majority of nonfamily board members will increase the probability of greater performance, the key driver of success is a *combination* of highly qualified family and nonfamily board members who represent complementary experience, skills, and perspective.

Starting with a family-only board, Granger and Associates, a waste and energy company, made steady progress over the first two generations. However, as business demands grew, opportunities became more complex, and capital needs increased, it became clear the family would benefit from outside points of view. One challenge was that none of the eight family directors was eager to step down. After they received in-depth education regarding the value of outside directors, one family member agreed to exit the board, recognizing that it was for the collective good of the family and the business. Two other family members resigned somewhat in protest, yet subsequently became believers in the blended family/independents governance model. Along with enduring some family pain, it took an open, innovative mind-set to promote the board's evolution. It's important to remember that change is relative. With regard to governance, some families may have had outside board members for generations, while others are just becoming accustomed to the idea. For the latter group, the inclusion of independent directors is indeed a new approach, and one that encourages other forms of change across the firm.

To implement the new approach, the Grangers used a task force to create an effective blend of family and nonfamily board members. The task force used strict qualification criteria, including deep experience/knowledge of the solid waste and renewable energy industries, to identify independent director candidates. Concurrently, the task force applied a less stringent set of criteria to assess family members. Today, the Granger family is happy to have a board with four family members and three outside directors, and they are benefiting from board members' complementary viewpoints.

Rotation and Retirement

Rotation and replacement of board directors through a combination of term limits and mandated retirement ensure a steady flow of fresh ideas and perspective, preventing the board from becoming stagnant. Additionally, agreed-upon terms of office induce the chair or the owning family to review director performance periodically. If there are term limits, the downside is that they may motivate effective directors to leave before management or owners want them to. The goal in structuring board terms should be to maximize both freshness and stability. On the one hand, the board should remain relevant and responsive to the company's changing needs. On the other hand, board structure should also afford directors an opportunity to gain a long-term perspective on the business and in-depth knowledge of its owners' values, temperament, and goals. When the family board members of the Behler Young Company, a Midwestern provider of heating and cooling products and services, heard that two longtime independent directors were opting not to renew their terms, they were energized to begin a search process for new members with a "non-status quo" approach to governance. Soon the search landed two directors with fresh and complementary perspectives, as the board had hoped.

Establishing a mandatory retirement age for board members has similar pros and cons. On the plus side, a mandatory retirement age facilitates a graceful transition for more senior board members. On the negative side, because greater age is not synonymous with lower involvement or insight—and may actually relate to deeper knowledge of the company and its industry—forced retirement may result in the loss of highly valuable directors. Transom Security faced this dilemma, as its board had four advisors in their 70s and 80s. Terms of two or three years would have allowed them to assess the need for change earlier, while a mandatory retirement age would have rendered tenure-related decisions unnecessary. A creative option is to find a supporting role for an aging yet strongly contributing board member. For example, instead of retiring John Mellowes from the board of Charter Manufacturing, cited in chapter 6, he was made Chairman *Emeritus*, acting as a senior ambassador for the company, while visiting plants and attending high-profile industry events.

Board Evaluation

A robust board evaluation process ensures a well-functioning, active, and involved board. Systematic evaluation uncovers and addresses issues related to board function and individual director contributions. Some families have standardized board evaluation processes, while others take a more casual approach.

Assessment of directors should account for the fact that advisors who are paid a retainer, such as lawyers and accountants, are not generally considered purely independent board members. The paid advisors earn ongoing service fees, whereas other outside advisors working only on board governance activity should be able to discuss important topics, including as related to innovation, from a fully unbiased position. Similarly, some family enterprises ask their family business consultants to attend board meetings, allowing them to observe proceedings and provide input—here again, assessment of the consultant's value is important. Another creative technique to gain expertise is to have an attorney or accountant serve as an officer. Since an officer of the company does not have to be a board member, some family firms have elected an attorney as secretary or an outside accountant as treasurer, again assessing these individuals' contributions carefully.

FAMILY COUNCIL

A family council, typically composed of family members who do not work in or are not employed by the business, but are not on the board, can capture the family's voice and communicate their needs and concerns to the board. This entity can help develop guiding documents, like the family constitution, which includes key policies or guidelines, such as those related to family member employment or compensation. Although family councils are often misunderstood as voting entities, they are not; they provide influence by voice, rather than vote. Importantly, their voice can be supportive of the innovation and risk-taking needed to help make meaningful changes at the business.

Generally, the family council is an ideal forum in which to cover three key areas: business updates, social/fun events, and family business education. Innovative family councils have created unique social and education opportunities for family members. One family we know holds an annual family meeting at the founder's ranch, where they provide "only-in-this-family" experiences for all ages. Riding horses, talking around the campfire, and fishing in a nearby stream set a wonderful stage for family bonding and discussion of important shareholder topics. They also take it a step further by bringing in team-building facilitators to run exercises, like the trust fall, which teach family members about living their values.

Some large family enterprises establish an ownership council to hear regularly from their large shareholder pools, especially when few family shareholders serve on the board. An ownership council can be especially useful when the number of shareholders passes 50 and the family council may become unable to address ownership matters adequately. As with the family council, the ownership council can be an important source of ideas and support for innovation.

EXECUTIVE TEAM

The official role of the executive team is to develop and execute business strategy. Governance oversight is formally the charter of the board of directors and other governance bodies discussed above. The chart below presents broad responsibility areas for executives and board members, to differentiate the roles for most family businesses.

Executive Team	Board of Directors
1. *Create* Strategic Business Plan	1. *Approve* Strategic Business Plan
2. *Create* a conprehensive strategic picture for Charter (the long term vision)	2. *Approve* long-term vision
	3. *Evaluate* President's performance annually
3. *Execute* the approved Plan	4. *Challenge* Executive Team with concepts, input from other companies, and new ideas.

Yet, as the people who know the business best, executives do play a key governance role. The board looks to executives to provide leadership for the company, including setting its culture. Just as for the board, an effective blend of family and nonfamily executives often drives long-term family business innovation and continuity. Forward-thinking families take an innovative approach to attracting and retaining nonfamily executives in order to benefit the business's performance and governance. An Upper Michigan family business advertised in *Field and Stream* magazine to invite prospective executives to leave the hustle and bustle of major metropolitan areas and come north to enjoy more time outdoors and with family. They successfully lured several candidates using this innovative measure and others, including phantom stock incentives.

Family and nonfamily executives can collaborate to tackle difficult decision-making. Of particular value can be a "behind-the-scenes" nonfamily executive who excels at cutting to the chase on strategic and tactical decisions, while incorporating the strengths and insights of family managers. Like Fred Mcalley of Transom Security, this person acts as the trusted confidant, sounding board, facilitator, corporate conscience, supporter, and challenger. He or she must be objective, tough minded, consistent, and above all deeply dedicated to the betterment of the entire company and the family. Such a nonfamily executive is the stabilizing force that balances the approach of family executives, while helping them shine. Thus innovative approaches to finding such executives are crucial, and one of their key sources of return is the executive's role in ongoing innovation.

SEVEN FAMILY BUSINESS TERRITORIES AND THEIR IMPACT ON GOVERNANCE

Understanding where family members fit into the family enterprise system can enhance development of an effective governance structure. The now well-established 3-Circle model presented earlier (including circles for family, business (employees), and owners) can be broken down further to illuminate the specific roles of each family member, executive, and board member. The overlaps and unshared spaces among the three groups represented by the circles create a complex system with seven distinct territories in which to place each individual (see figure 7.4). The overarching challenge is managing all three spheres simultaneously and symbiotically.

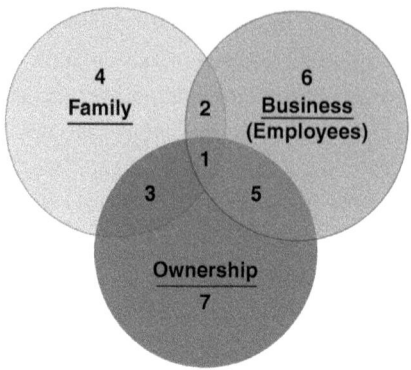

FIGURE 7.4 The Family Business Territories

Innovative family leaders have learned to apply business acumen and family sensitivity to make this a reality, resulting in productive, harmonious interactions.[4] In line with this chapter's theme, getting roles and relationships within and among the territories right can reflect creative approaches and is also important for supporting organization-wide innovation.

Members of the Transom family and enterprise may be categorized as follows.

1. *Family, Employees, Owners*: Walter, George, Elizabeth
2. *Family and Employee (but not Owner)*: Ron (Valerie's spouse), Bill, Alicia (Bill's daughter)
3. *Family and Owners (but not Employees)*: Millie, Lucille, Cheryl, Valerie, Jeff
4. *Family only*: 3 third-generation spouses, 4 second-generation spouses, 24 fourth-generation members
5. *Employee and Owner (but not Family)*: Transom President Fred Mcalley
6. *Employee only*: Transom's Executive & Management Team
7. *Owner only*: Investor in Transom real estate LLC

As discussed below, each territory is associated with a specific identity and set of challenges for the people who inhabit it, and these features have implications for how the family enterprise will be governed. You can think of this practical analysis and application of the 3-Circle model as an incremental innovation in helping families improve governance through a deeper understanding of the system in which they participate.

1. *Family Member, Employee, and Owner*

   This is the epicenter, where the three spheres intersect, home to those who are simultaneously family members, employees (often executives), and owners. In a small business they are called "owner-operators." In a larger enterprise, the family members in this space have tremendous pressure to ensure that the business runs successfully, that owners secure a reasonable return, and that the greater family stays unified. This core territory is associated with the greatest control over the family business, and thus it is where the greatest burden of responsibility falls.

   Residents of this territory must wear many hats. In fact, some family leaders we know express the specific role they are playing at a given time by *literally* wearing a different hat, labeled family member, business leader, or owner. In the context of a given meeting, interaction, or topic, the family member will slip on the appropriate hat. Of course, there are times when the family leader must wear all three hats, literally or metaphorically, because it is far from easy to separate these roles.

   Other innovative ways in which families have managed this demanding role include making explicit what percentage of their time is reasonable to spend in each sphere—for example, 75 percent on business/management, 15 percent on family matters, 10 percent on ownership. The challenge is adhering to these guidelines. One family chair/president/CEO shares a pie chart at each board meeting that indicates his time spent in each role since the last meeting, and seeks input on how he could improve the proportions as needed. In many instances, a family may hire a nonfamily executive such as a COO to run the day-to-day business, freeing family executives to focus on strategy, family development, and ownership issues.

2. *Family and Employee (but not Owner)*

   The intersection of family and employee/manager (but not ownership) is a common residence for younger-generation family members.

Spouses frequently occupy this space, as well. It is critical territory, often inhabited by family members who have a great impact on business performance. As such, this space can be marked by awkwardness, as the family members within it provide value to the business, but do not share the rewards of ownership (yet). The situation is made even more challenging if there is no clear path for ownership succession.

A simple but still innovative way to handle individuals in this space is to treat them like any other employee with regard to performance, creating a culture of meritocracy. That would include policies related to performance reviews (such as annual 360-degree evaluations) and, of course, compensation. On the other hand, because family employees may represent future owners and/or executives, it is appropriate to include opportunities for their learning and development. Examples might be exposure to key meetings (management and board), internal mentorship programs (available to nonfamily employees as well), education opportunities (such as degree and certification programs, which are available to nonfamily employees as well), and representation of the family at community events.

3. *Family and Owner (but not Employee)*
   This is often a more challenging territory because individuals within it may not know the business well, but still have a substantial financial (and emotional) stake in it. Innovative ways to handle this role include
   - developing family governance entities, such as a family council, to provide individuals in this territory a more formal, collective voice; an ownership council may be appropriate if there are 50 or more shareholders, as discussed earlier;
   - recruiting family members to develop an active family newsletter or website;
   - encouraging family members to attend board meetings, to become more knowledgeable, responsible, and potentially active shareholders.

4. *Family only*
   This is typically the domain of family members such as spouses and next-generation adults and children who are not yet shareholders or

may never be. Although many may be pursuing satisfying outside careers or interests, they tend to be pulled into the family business by family meetings, financial issues, or other matters. Innovative approaches here include

- developing a family code of conduct that includes guidelines for when it is *not* appropriate to discuss the business (such as family social outings);
- creating experiential learning opportunities for family members, including those related to philanthropy;
- encouraging family council service;
- asking for volunteers to create the story of the family's history, values, and legacy.

5. *Employee and Owner (but not Family)*

These are often key employees who have either bought into the business or earned ownership through incentive programs. The family may have provided stock options or a minority position for executives with a strong record of contribution, such as Transom's president, Fred Mcalley. These people, while not bloodline family members, become part of the business family because of their ownership stake and value. Innovative ways to optimize this role include

- having such executives attend part of family/shareholder meetings to share their perspective on the business and its performance;
- providing clear means of stock redemption to incentivize executives to remain at the family business, yet avoid making executives feel handcuffed beyond initial ownership periods;
- empowering share-owning executives to help select outside board members;
- providing ongoing performance incentives that are tied to profitable growth; for example, one firm offers a graduated bonus program that rewards 10 percent or greater revenue growth and 5 percent or greater operating profit growth.

6. *Employee only*

This territory typically includes the nonfamily management, but you can think of this sphere as including the majority of people working in most family businesses; they are neither family nor owners. The firms with the most motivating practices and cultures tend to make individuals in this space *feel like family*. This emphasis has won some family firms recognition as the best workplaces for employees in a region or even the entire country. The Marvin Companies—a fourth-generation windows and door company in Minnesota—have many employees who claim they feel part of the family. Stew Leonard's grocery stores in the Northeast United States continue to earn "Best Place to Work" awards, based largely on their success in creating an atmosphere where employees are proud to contribute.

Other innovative practices to engage residents of this sphere include
- celebrations—recognizing great performance at company meetings and other events;
- phantom stock, value appreciating rights (VARs), or stock appreciating rights (SARs)—providing key employees with an opportunity to participate in the business's growth value;
- participation in board meetings—allowing key executives to attend and often present important topics during board meetings;
- education—educating employees on governance and ownership;
- ESOPs—maintaining an employee stock ownership program (ESOP) that allows employees to become minority shareholders.

7. *Owner only*

In some cases, the family may have an investor, often a silent owner, who has put money into the business to help the family achieve a certain level of growth and return on investment. In the GRSS auto supply family business, for example, the family gave a silent partner 40 percent ownership for his initial investment. A key consideration for this role is the development of a clear exit plan outlining how the nonfamily investors can redeem shares. The GRSS Company developed an amenable way to buy out the outside shareholder. Other ways of optimizing such relationships include keeping the outside owner up to speed on what is happening in the business through regular updates and granting them "observatory rights" to observe executive meetings, board meetings, and other important activities.

BEWARE THESE PITFALLS

- **Role Confusion**—When a person does not understand the role he or she plays in the family business system, he or she can create significant dysfunction. Take steps to ensure that everyone in every sphere—family, business, owner, and their overlapping territories—understands his or her role in the system and how it can add the most value to the enterprise.
- **Ignoring Board Member Input**—Whether the family business has an advisory or a fiduciary board, it needs to heed innovative ideas from outside board members. Failing to do so will result in the loss of valuable opportunities and, ultimately, strong board directors.
- **Family Council Irrelevance**—To have a meaningful voice in the family business, the family council should focus on relevant topics, such as family employment policy, plans for family meetings, and suggestions for family education. If the family council has few members and/or revolves only around the "fun" aspects of family (such as reunions), it will lose value for the system.

THINGS TO REMEMBER

- Thoughtful, innovative approaches to family business governance can enhance business performance and family satisfaction; getting governance right is about optimizing relationships among family members, shareholders, and managers, which can be depicted by the 3-Circle model; governance-related measures can both reflect innovation and serve to support broader innovation firm wide.
- The three entities with the most influence on governance are the board of directors, the family council, and the executive team
- The *board of directors* is best served by a mix of independent outsiders (ideally the majority) and family members; boards typically evolve from a "paper" board to an advisory board to a board with fiduciary responsibility, with five to nine members as the optimal number;

rotating/replacing board members and evaluating them regularly are best practices.
- *Family councils* capture the family's voice and communicate their needs to the board, including matters related to family member employment, the council can also take responsibility for social events and family education.
- *Ownership councils* are especially useful for family businesses with over 50 shareholders, where a family council might be insufficient.
- The *executive team* develops business strategy and also influences governance by leading the company and setting its culture.
- Based on the 3-Circle model, members of a family enterprise system can fall into seven unique territories, each with a specific identity and set of challenges; building awareness of each territories features and best practices is crucial.
- Governance-related pitfalls include role confusion and ignoring board member input.

Chapter 8

Moving Innovation Forward: Concluding Thoughts

"Now I see how smart Grandpa was to develop new technology for making snow and to change our distribution from independent reps to a direct sales force," Edward said to his mother while they enjoyed lunch in the break room at the family's Wisconsin-based snowmaking equipment business. Edward, age 28 and a third-generation member, had recently joined the business as a sales representative, and his inside view helped him understand the impact of the founder's innovative approach. Edward's mother agreed, "Thanks to my father's foresight, your generation has many opportunities to work in the business and take it to the next level."

* * *

It is uplifting to read family businesses stories that demonstrate the power of change. When it becomes clear to incoming family members that it took some truly innovative moves to create, grow, and sustain the family business, they understand the critical nature of innovation more deeply than ever before. When rising generations embrace innovation as an essential element in driving meaningful change and get excited about stewarding the family assets with this component as a guiding force, then the enterprise's odds of prospering across future generations increase dramatically.

LOOKING BACK: A SUMMARY OF THE BOOK

My goal here has been to *inspire enterprising families to focus more energy and resources on innovation throughout their family businesses, and to provide them some ideas for creative directions to pursue on multiple dimensions.* Let's take a look back at the earlier chapters to understand how they speak to this objective.

Our journey began with chapter 1, which described in detail the innovation *drivers* in a family business, especially those that set family firms apart from other businesses. From the well-known family trait of a time long-term horizon to the lesser-known but equally important driver of incremental innovation, multiple distinct characteristics drive innovation in a family business and can collectively produce meaningful change. Chapter 2 discussed how these drivers fit into an overall *culture of innovation* in family firms. Creating an innovative culture can infuse an organization with a mind-set that embraces change rather than fights it. Not surprisingly, promoting a culture of innovation is tough, risky, and at times confusing. However, as one senior entrepreneurial family leader proclaimed, "developing a culture of innovation is not only necessary; it is more exciting than just sticking with the status quo." Enterprising families use innovative cultures to create new products, services, and processes and develop creative practices in other areas in order to prosper from generation to generation.

Chapter 3 built on the previous material by highlighting the area where families focus most of their innovation resources: *product and service offerings, new ventures, and start-ups,* or what are traditionally thought of as "innovation." Selecting or customizing a specific process and using a disciplined approach increases the probability of a steady stream of value-generating offerings. Chapter 4 described the need to think carefully about *funding and measuring innovation.* Aiming resources—money and other assets—at supporting innovation and measuring its progress heightens the chance of more meaningful change across dimensions. Since the younger generation drives the future, including progress that is led by adaptation, chapter 5 underscored ways that the upcoming generation can *reinnovate* the family business, with a focus on getting next-generation members involved in innovative thinking and practices in multiple areas.

Chapters 6 and 7 took a slightly different tack to address the critical importance of the supporting role of *succession and governance* as related to innovation. While there are innovative steps that family firms have undertaken and can undertake to transition ownership/leadership and to govern the business, succession and governance are important parts of the foundation needed for healthy innovation. Successful transition among leaders and owners and thoughtful governance of the relationships among family, management, and ownership is crucial to maximize the value of innovation.

Collectively, this content has been written to present a clearer view of the scope of innovation in the family business. At the same time, it can serve as a canvas on which to paint your own firm's detailed innovation picture.

LOOKING FORWARD: THE CRITICAL ROLE OF INNOVATION

As we have discussed, family enterprises have represented the dominant form of business system worldwide for centuries. An important question, then, is whether they can continue to be successful and the role innovation will play in their success. Multiple lines of evidence gathered by FBCG and other organizations suggest that innovation adds significant value to family firms, not only in the financial sense but also as a route to greater family continuity, a value with great significance to society as a whole.

While there is strong evidence of the link between innovation and family business value, there are clear areas that require further understanding and research, in order to enhance this intersection further. While innovation does occur within family businesses, as the multiple examples in this book suggest, it still tends to happen more out of necessity or opportunistically, rather than deliberately or as the product of a firm-wide focus on meaningful change. Can innovation become more of an intentional, systematic practice? We are learning from observation of another family business factor—governance—that a company's more deliberate efforts for improvement in a specific area does enhance overall performance. FBCG studies indicate that appointing independent outside members to family business boards drives positive impact throughout the family business. As a result, more family firms are actively assessing their governance practices and seeking to add independent board members. Likewise, family firms with a written strategic plan, rather than a verbal plan or no plan at all, tend to perform better. So it's reasonable to expect that a family firm's efforts of being more deliberate about innovation will drive greater performance. Being more deliberate means applying the suggestions laid out in this book: creating a culture of innovation, establishing an innovation process, funding and measuring innovation, helping the next generation reinnovate, and ensuring that succession and governance processes support innovation.

This is, of course, easier said (or thought) than done. Since the field of innovation in family business is still young, there exist many interpretations of what innovation means, and it can be tough to get your hands around it even after reading a book like this. However, becoming more intentional about learning, understanding, and applying innovation should help the performance of family businesses and, in turn, long-term continuity.

As a closing thought, consider a number of hypotheses that can be tested, as related to innovation in family business. Further evidence can help validate these predictions and enhance the body of knowledge, including research and stories, that family businesses can access to promote their own innovation.

- Greater overall application of innovation drives greater value—financial and nonfinancial—for family businesses.
- Innovation is one of the most important driving forces for sustaining family business performance and continuity.
- On average, incremental innovation is more likely to help family firms sustain long-term prosperity than groundbreaking innovation.
- Continuous innovation drives family business continuity.

This is fertile ground on which researchers and practitioners can collaborate to generate meaningful findings and applications for family firms interested in innovation.

LET'S CONTINUE THE CONVERSATION

Family business members tend to learn best from other family business members. The 50 family stories and scenarios described in this book have, hopefully, inspired creative thinking about innovative ways to address myriad family business situations, from leadership succession and new family ventures to clever estate planning and next-generation development. Still, the innovation stories in this book are just a tiny fraction of the many more examples out there, including yours. We are always interested in capturing and communicating family business innovation stories, to help others learn from them. Please send your own firm's stories to me at *schmieder@thefbcg.com*.

Remember: the most important thing is to maintain an open mind-set about innovation and to try different approaches, learning from each. I wish you the very best on your family business innovation journey, wherever you are in the process.

Notes

Introduction: Creating the Future—Leading Through Innovation

1. Robert G. Cooper, *Winning at New Products* (Boston: Addison-Wesley, 1993).
2. The Boston Consulting Group, "Our Innovation Competencies," http://www.bcg.com/expertise_impact/capabilities/innovation/competencies.aspx.
3. Family Firm Institute, "Global Data Points," http://www.ffi.org/?page=globaldatapoints.

1 The Family Business Difference: Capitalizing on Family Innovation

1. Sylvie Laforet, *Innovation in Small Family Businesses* (Cheltenham, UK: Edward Elgar Publishing, 2012), 2.
2. Alfredo De Massis, Federico Frattini, Emanuele Pizzurno, and Lucio Cassia, "Product Innovation in Family versus Nonfamily Firms: An Exploratory Analysis," *Journal of Small Business Management* (2013).
3. Kikkoman's Mogi Family Creed, University of Massachusetts Amherst website, http://www.umass.edu/fambiz/articles/values_culture/kikkoman.html (accessed June 2, 2014).
4. John L. Ward, "Introduction," in Joseph Tapies and John L. Ward (eds), *Family Values and Value Creation* (New York: Palgrave Macmillan, 2008), 3.
5. For a discussion of strategic experimentation in family business, see John L. Ward and Craig E. Aronoff, *Preparing Your Family Business for Strategic Change* (New York: Palgrave Macmillan, 2010).
6. Welch Allyn company website, "Submit an Idea," https://www.welchallyn.com/about/innovation/submit-an-idea.htm (accessed February 10, 2014).
7. "Innovation 2010: A Return to Prominence and the New World Order," Boston Consulting Group, April 2010.

2 Structured Chaos: Creating a Culture of Innovation

1. *The American Heritage Dictionary of the English Language* (Boston: Houghton Mifflin Harcourt, 2000).
2. Randel S. Carlock and John L. Ward, *When Family Businesses Are Best* (New York: Palgrave Macmillan,, 2010).
3. Amy Schuman, Stacy Stutz, and John L. Ward, *Family Business as Paradox* (New York: Palgrave Macmillan, 2010).
4. Rita Gunther McGrath, "How the Growth Outliers Do It," *Harvard Business Review*, January-February 2012.
5. Charles O'Reilly and Michael Tushman, "Ambidexterity as a Dynamic Capability: Resolving the Innovator's Dilemma," *Research in Organizational Behavior* 28 (2008): 185–206.
6. Chris Zook, *Unstoppable: Finding Hidden Assets to Renew the Core and Fuel Profitable Growth* (Boston: Harvard Business School Press, Boston, 2007).
7. Robert Cooper, *Winning at New Products* (New York: Basic Books, 2011).
8. Byrne Electrical Specialists, "The Byrne Story," https://www.byrne-electrical.com/Home/Story (accessed February 4, 2014).
9. Specific information about Schwinn from Judith Crown and Glenn Coleman, *No Hands: The Rise and Fall of the Schwinn Bicycle Company* (New York: Henry Holt, 1996)
10. Specific information about Ford from Bryce Hoffman, *American Icon: Alan Mulally and the Fight to Save the Ford Motor Company* (New York: Crown Business, 2013).
11. James D. Smith III, "Harvest Seasons: Most Runs-Batted-In with Fewest Home Runs Since 1920," *SABR Research Journals Archive*, http://research.sabr.org/journals/harvest-seasons-most-runs-batted-in (accessed June 4, 2014).
12. Scott Edinger, "4 Steps for Creating a Culture of Innovation" (CEO Briefing Newsletter, January 2013). See Edinger Consulting Group website, www.edingergroup.com.
13. For example, NYU Professor Adam Alter's *Drunk Tank Pink: And Other Unexpected Forces That Shape How We Think, Feel, and Behave* (New York: Penguin, 2012).

3 New Products and Services: Creating Value with Innovative Offerings

1. Hannah Meckstroth (University of Notre Dame intern), Survey of Advisors of the Family Business Consulting Group, 2012.
2. Frank Bacon and Thomas Butler, *Planned Innovation* (Ann Arbor: Industrial Development Division, Institute of Science and Technology, the University of Michigan, 1981), 9.

3. Christian Caspar, Ana Karina Dias, and Heinz-Peter Elstrodt, "The Five Attributes of Enduring Family Business," *McKinsey Quarterly*, January 2010, http://www.mckinsey.com/insights/organization/the_five_attributes_of_enduring_family_businesses (accessed February 25, 2014).
4. Ibid.
5. John L. Ward, "Better Built to Last Longer," *Campden Families in Business*, 24, Jan./Feb. 2006.
6. Robert Wolcott and Michael Lippitz, *Grow from Within* (New York: McGraw-Hill, 2010).
7. Kohler, "About Us," Kohler website, http://believe.kohler.com/about-us (retrieved February 26, 2014).
8. Michael Carney, "Corporate Governance and Competitive Advantage in Family Controlled Firms," *Entrepreneurship Theory and Practice*, 29 (2005): 249.
9. Robert Cooper, *Winning at New Products* (New York: Basic Books, 1993).
10. Greg Stevens, WinOvations; see website at www.winovations.com.
11. Frank Bacon and Thomas Butler, *Planning Innovation* (New York: Free Press, 2007).
12. Greg Stevens, James Burley, and Richard Divine, "Creativity Business Discipline = Higher Profits Faster from New Product Development," *Journal of Product Innovation Management*, 16(5) (1999): 455–468. Also see http://www.myersbriggs.org/ for more information on the dimensions and applications of the Myers-Briggs Trait Inventory.
13. For more on IDEO, see the firm's website: www.ideo.com.
14. IDEO, "About Us," http://www.ideo.com/about/ (accessed February 28, 2014).
15. Fernando Trias De Bes and Philip Kotler, *Winning at Innovation* (New York: Palgrave Macmillan, 2011).
16. Ibid., inside cover jacket.

4 Money and Metrics: Funding and Measuring Innovation

1. Joe Schmieder, "FBCG Survey of Select Family businesses Associated with Young Presidents Organization and World Presidents Organization," 2012.
2. FBCG client database.
3. The Conference Board CEO Challenge® 2014: People and Performance, http://www.conference-board.org/subsites/index.cfm?id=14514 (accessed June 9, 2014).
4. "Assessing Innovation Metrics: McKinsey Global Survey Results," *The McKinsey Quarterly*, November 2008.

5. Robert C. Wolcott and Michael J. Lippitz, *Grow from Within* (New York: McGraw-Hill, 2010), 126–127.

5 The Next Generation: Reinnovating the Family Business

1. Charles Bagli, "Flipping a Coin, Dividing an Empire," *New York Times*, October 31, 2009, http://www.nytimes.com/2009/11/01/business/01real.html?pagewanted=all&_r=0 (accessed May 11, 2014).
2. Greg Stevens, James Burley, and Richard Divine, "Creativity Business Discipline = Higher Profits Faster from New Product Development," *Journal of Product Innovation Management*, 16(5) (1999): 455–468.
3. Henry William Chesebrough, "The Era of Open Innovation," *MIT Sloan Management Review*, 44(3) (2003): 35–41.

6 Leadership and Ownership Transitions: Ensuring Succession Supports Innovation

1. John L. Ward, "The Succession Task Force: A Tool for Managing Uncertain Times," *The Family Business Advisor*, November 2008, 1.
2. Mike Ramsey, "Henry Ford's Great-Great Grandchildren Join the Family Business," *The Wall Street Journal*, June 26, 2013, http://online.wsj.com/news/articles/SB10001424127887323734304578545431695518150 (accessed March 21, 2014).
3. Andrew W. Mayoras and Danielle Mayoras, *Trial & Heirs: Famous Fortune Fights!* (Long Beach, CA: Wise Circle Books, 2009).

7 Governance: Overseeing Key Relationships to Support Innovation

1. Craig E. Aronoff and John L. Ward, *Family Business Governance: Maximizing Family and Business Potential* (New York: Palgrave Macmillan, 2010); Jennifer M. Pendergast, John L. Ward, and Stephanie Brun de Pontet, *Building a Successful Family Business Board* (New York: Palgrave Macmillan, 2011).
2. Jennifer M. Pendergast, John L. Ward, and Stephanie Brun de Pontet, *Building a Successful Family Business Board* (New York: Palgrave Macmillan, 2011).
3. Jennifer M. Pendergast, John L. Ward, and Stephanie Brun de Pontet, *Building a Successful Family Business Board* (New York: Palgrave Macmillan, 2011).
4. Business Families Foundation, Family Business 101 course material, 2013, www.businessfamiles.org.

About the Author

Joe Schmieder is a Principal Consultant of the Family Business Consulting Group specializing in family business succession planning and strategic business planning. He is a strong advocate for incorporating innovation into family businesses, blending family and nonfamily executives into effective leadership teams, developing the next generation leaders, creating effective governance structures (boards of directors and family councils), and facilitating family meetings.

Joe earned his Masters of International Management degree from Thunderbird Global School of International Management and a Bachelor of Science degree from Central Michigan University. In addition to his consulting practice, Joe serves as an adjunct professor at Notre Dame University teaching Family Enterprise Strategy courses.

Joe serves, or has served, on a number of family business and community boards, including: Burke E. Porter Machinery Company, Custer Workplace Interiors, Via Design, The Mayline Group, EJ, YPO-WPO, St. Mary's Foundation and Juvenile Diabetes Research Foundation.

Index

3-Circle model, 92–93, 99–100, 105–6
3M, 58–59

A-to-F model, 45–46, 50
activators, 46
  see also A-to-F model
advisors (FBCG), 35, 70, 79–80, 85, 93, 97
advisory board, 81, 90, 93–94, 105
allocation challenges, 53
Allyn, William G., 12
ambidexterity, 21
Amway, 6, 68
ArtPrize, 68
AS Corporation, 69

B&B, 15–18, 21, 24, 28–30
Bacon, Frank, 36
Behler Young Company, 96
Beretta, 20
Bissell, Inc., 78
board of directors
  evaluation, 96–97
  example, 89–93
  executive team and, 98–99
  family council and, 97–98
  funding and, 51–52
  ignoring input from, 105
  innovation and, 25, 32, 110
  leveraging governance bodies and, 28
  measuring and, 57–58
  next generation and, 62, 67–68
  overview, 93–94
  responsibilities, 99, 101–5
  rotation and retirement, 95–96
  seeking innovative members, 25
  size and composition, 94–95
  succession and, 79–81, 84–85, 87
Boeing, 23, 81
Brandon family, 73–75, 82–83
Brown family, 15–17, 24, 28
Brown, Tim, 45
browsers, 46
  see also A-to-F model
budgets, 29, 53, 55, 58
Butler, Thomas, 36
Byrne Electrical Specialists, 10–11, 22–23, 25

capital markets, independence from, 11–12
Cargill, 38, 59
Carter family, 89
celebrations, 104
Cemex, 26
charitable lead trust (CLT), 85
charitable remainder trust (CRT), 85
Charter Manufacturing Company, 78–79, 96
charters, board of directors and, 98
Chevy Chase Land Company, 28
communication, 5, 28–29, 32, 57, 97, 106, 111
compensation, 29, 67, 91, 97, 102, 106
conventional thinking, 5, 12, 14

Cooper, Robert, 21, 41
cooperation, 6
Corning, 41
creativity
　culture of, 45–46
　funding and, 5, 54
　innovation and, 15–22, 25–26, 29–30, 59
　new products/services and, 34, 39, 44–45
　next generation and, 65, 68–69
　roles/responsibilities and, 96–97, 100
　success and, 2, 10
　succession and, 79, 84–85
　talent and, 29
creators, 46
　see also A-to-F model
crisis succession exercise, 82–83
Critikon, 36–37
cross-functional teams, 29
culture, innovation and, 18–23
Custer Workplace Interiors, 34, 81

debt
　avoiding, 54
　capital markets and, 11
　equity and, 11–12, 39
　operating with, 3
　taking on, 7. 54
　transitioning ownership and, 27
decision-making, 4, 13, 20, 70, 77–78, 82, 87, 93, 99
design thinking, 45, 50
developers, 46–47
　see also A-to-F model
developing next generation, 27–28
DeVos, Rich, 6, 68
Digital Age, 8
Disney, 57
distributions, 11, 54–56, 60, 74, 84, 89
Douglas family, 1–5, 8–10
Dow Chemical, 44

Drucker, Peter, 67
Dundee Enterprises, 73–74, 76, 79, 82–83
DuPont, 36–37, 41
Duration Ag Products, 2–6, 10, 76
dynasty trust, 85

education, 28–29, 32, 51–53, 64, 66, 71, 90, 95, 97, 102, 104–6
Ed-Zone, 51–55, 59
Elghanayan family, 65, 86
Emerging Business Accelerator (EBA), 59
employee stock ownership program (ESOP), 104
entering the business, 66, 78
equity
　debt-to-equity ratio, 11–12, 39
　private-equity-owned firms, 22
ESPN, 56–57
estate planning, 3, 35, 84–85, 111
estate taxes, 22, 74
executive team, 16, 79, 92, 98–99, 105
executors, 46–47
　see also A-to-F model
exiting the business, 66–67
experimental tolerance, 12, 14
expertise, 67, 97
Exxon, 41

Facebook, 86
facilitators, 46–47, 65–66, 98–99
　see also A-to-F model
Family Business Consulting Group (FBCG), 10, 22, 35, 47, 54, 63, 70, 77, 93–94, 109–11
family businesses
　differences of, 4
　drivers of innovation in, 36–40
　experimental tolerance, 12
　incremental vs. radical innovation, 7–9

independence from capital
  markets, 11–12
leadership, 13–14
longer-term horizon, 9–10
overview, 1–3
personal attachments and, 5–7
shared values, 10–11
success and, 10–11
family employment provisions, 27
family leadership, 13–14
Field and Stream magazine, 99
FLP, 111–12
Ford family, 23, 25, 81, 84–86
formal innovation process, 30
Frey, Ellie, 66
funding innovation
  allocation challenges, 53
  diversification, 56–57
  examples of, 55–56
  measuring, 57–59
  pitfalls, 59–60
  where to find, 54–55

games, 65
generation-skipping trust, 85
gift-of-genius myth, 36
gift of interest in family limited
  partnership, 85
globalization, 22–23
Google, 26, 38
governance
  3-Circle mode, 92
  board evaluation, 96–97
  board of directors, 93–97
  categorization of employees, 100
  executive team, 98–99
  family business territories, 99–104
  family council, 97–98
  overview, 89–93
  pitfalls, 105
  rotation and retirement, 95–96
  simplified governance structure, 94

size and composition of boards,
  94–95
Graduate, The, 70
Granger and Associates, 95
grantor retained annuity trust
  (GRAT), 85–86
Great Depression, 33–34
Grounder family, 51–52, 55–56, 58
groupthink, 87–88
Grow from Within (Wolcott and
  Lippitz), 38
GRSS Company, 104

Hearst family, 56–57, 84–85
Hendrick family, 9
human resources (HR), 30, 80, 91

IDEO, 45
incentives, 20, 54, 60, 99, 103
incremental development, 24, 38–39
independence from capital markets,
  11–12
ignoring board member input, 105–6
innovation
  balancing stability with, 26–27
  board members and, 25, 32
  budgets, 29
  creating culture of, 18–21
  defining as positive change, 25
  developing next generation, 27–28
  examples of, 26–28
  funding, 53–57
  high-potential items for building,
    28–30
  incremental, 7–9, 24
  key questions for building, 17
  leveraging governance bodies, 28
  measuring, 57–59
  making space for, 25–26
  micromanagement and, 24–25
  operations and, 30
  optimizing leadership, 27

INDEX

innovation—*Continued*
  overview, 15–17
  pitfalls to avoid, 30–31
  reasons for fostering, 21–23
  steps for creating, 24–26
  things to remember, 31–32
  transitioning ownership, 27
intentionally defective irrevocable trust (IDIT), 85
Internal Revenue Service (IRS), 86
irrevocable life insurance trust (ILIT), 85

Jackoboice family, 82
job descriptions, 29
Johnson & Johnson, 36

Kelley, David, 45
Key Strategic Focus Areas, 11
Kikkoman Soy Sauce, 10
knowledge building, 29
Kohler Company, 38–40
Kotler, Philip, 45–46

leadership
  decision-making, 13
  developing, 66–67
  innovation and, 24
  optimizing, 27
  transition of, 73–75, 77–83
Lencioni, Patrick, 67
letters of wishes, 87
leveraging governance bodies, 28
LLCs, 91, 100
longer-time horizons, 9–10, 14, 39–40
loose/tight leashes, 70–71
low leverage, 4, 11–12, 36–37, 39, 50
Loyola University, 65

macroeconomic trends, 21
Market Value Added (MVA) innovation framework, 47–48, 50

Marvin Companies, 104
Mcalley, Fred, 90, 99–100, 103
McGrath, Rita Gunther, 20
McKinsey, 37, 58
Mellowes, John A., 78, 96
Meyers Briggs personality test, 69
micromanagement, 24–25
mismeasurement of innovation, 60
modernization, 7
Mulally, Alan, 23, 81

naysayers, 31–32
new products and services
  A-to-F model, 45–47
  controlled risk-taking and, 37
  customer and supplier relationships, 36–37
  design thinking, 45
  drivers of, 36–40
  focus of family business innovation resources, 35
  importance of, 34–35
  incremental developments, 38–39
  innovation by business model, 49
  innovation processes, 40–47
  longer-term horizon, 39–40
  low leverage, 39
  MVA innovation framework, 47–48
  overview, 33–34
  pitfalls, 49–50
  Stage-Gate process, 41–42
  WinOvations, 41, 43–44
Newlands, Francis G., 28
Next Gen Peer Groups, 65–66
next generation
  developing, 65–66
  entering, working, exiting, 66–68
  family office and, 68–69
  innovation across generations, 63–65
  overview, 61–63

pitfalls, 70–71
selecting and nurturing innovation
    rainmakers, 69–70
nonfamily
  board of directors, 93–95
  employees, 102
  executives, 7–8, 20, 28, 54, 65, 74,
    77, 79–81, 93, 98–99, 101, 103
  firms, 4–5, 8–9, 13, 18, 24, 36–37
  shareholders, 84, 92, 104
not letting go, 70
Nucraft Furniture Company, 13

observatory rights, 104
Oliver Machinery Company, 33,
  35–38
Oliver Products Company, 40, 44, 80
operations, 30, 75, 79–80, 82
organizing principles, 29
outside support, 29
overexuberance, 59
ownership
  councils, 98, 102, 106
  family business and, 4
  governance and, 89–92, 98–104, 109
  innovation and, 35
  structure, 35
  succession, 22, 35, 73–76, 83–88
  transitioning, 3, 6, 20, 27, 31

Padnos Company, 79
past, holding onto, 49
performance plans, 29
personal attachments, 5–7
pet ideas, 49–50
phantom stock, 99, 104
philanthropy, 86, 90, 103
Pixar, 26
Planned Innovation, 40–41, 50
present, being trapped by, 70
Procter & Gamble, 41
process, innovation and, 30

Product Development and
  Management Association
  (PDMA), 55

qualified personal residence trust
  (QPRT), 85

rainmakers, 44, 69–70
Rawling family, 27–28
reinvestment, 14, 54–56, 60
retirement, 27, 80–81, 90, 95–96
revenue analysis and goals, 29
Robar family, 61–64
role confusion, 105–6
roles and relationships
  Employee and Owner (but not
    Family), 103
  Employee only, 103–4
  Family and Employee (but not
    Owner), 101–2
  Family and Owner (but not
    Employee), 102
  Family Member, Employee, and
    Owner, 101
  Family only, 102–3
  overview, 99–101
  Owner only, 104
  pitfalls, 105
rotation, 29, 95–96, 106

Safeway, 44
S.C. Johnson, 18–19
Schad, Matt, 13
Schwinn, 23
self-canceling installment note
  (SCIN), 85
shared values, 10–11, 14
shareholders, 6–7, 9, 24, 27–28, 51,
  54–56, 67, 74, 84, 86, 89, 92, 94,
  98, 102–6
social events, 97, 103, 106
social networking, 66

space, creating, 25–26
Sparkeology, 9
spouses, 82, 91, 100, 102
stability
 board of directors and, 96
 executives and, 99
 innovation and, 20–21, 26–27, 29, 31
 values and, 11, 29
Stage-Gate, 41–42, 50
Steelcase Corporation, 26, 86
Stevens, Greg, 44, 69
strategic business planning, 24, 76–77, 88, 98
success, defined, 10–11
succession
 challenge of, 75–76
 examples of, 82–85
 executive leadership and, 81
 foundation for, 76–77
 gifting to "unborn" children, 86
 incoming generation and, 81–82
 independent task force and, 79–81
 innovation ownership succession, 85–87
 leadership succession, 77–83
 outgoing generation and, 78–79
 overview, 73–75
 ownership succession, 83–87
 philanthropy and, 86
 pitfalls, 87
 random allocation of ownership, 86
supplier relationships, 36–37, 50
surveys, 30, 35, 54, 57–58, 94
symbols, stories, and messages, 28–29

Takemura, 69
talent and teens, 29
taxes, 22, 27, 74, 84–86

Transom Security Systems, 89–93, 96, 99–100, 103
Trias De Bes, Fernando, 45
trust, 5–6, 25, 32, 47, 98–99
trusts, 74, 84–86, 88
Tuthill family, 33–34, 36–37, 44
Tyvek, 37

value appreciating rights (VARs), 104
values
 board of directors and, 96
 family businesses and, 2, 4, 9
 family council and, 98
 governance and, 96, 103
 innovation and, 18–20, 63–64, 71
 personal ties, 6
 shared, 10–11, 14
 success and, 2, 10–11
 succession and, 75–78, 81, 87–88
 tradition and, 63–64, 71, 75
Van Andel, Jay, 6
variable compensation, 29
vision, 10–11, 18–19, 21, 23–27, 35–36, 39, 49, 61, 76, 84, 88, 98
visual reminders, 28

Ward, John L., 10, 20, 38, 80
wealth management, 35
Wee Folk, 23
Welch Allyn, 12
WinOvations, 41, 43–44, 50, 69
Worden Company, 9

Young Presidents Organization (YPO), 65–66

Zuckerburg, Mark, 86

ADDITIONAL BESTSELLING BOOKS FOR YOUR FAMILY BUSINESS LIBRARY

$23.00 | 978-0-230-11100-4

$23.00 | 978-0-230-11106-6

$23.00 | 978-0-230-11230-8

$23.00 | 978-0-230-34216-3

$23.00 | 978-1-137-27460-1

$23.00 | 978-1-137-38623-6

$55.00 | 978-0-230-11219-3

$40.00 | 978-1-137-28089-3

$40.00 | 978-0-230-11154-7

palgrave macmillan | PROFESSIONAL BUSINESS

Learn more at
www.palgrave.com/professionalbusiness
or follow us on Twitter @PalgraveBiz

GPSR Compliance
The European Union's (EU) General Product Safety Regulation (GPSR) is a set
of rules that requires consumer products to be safe and our obligations to
ensure this.

If you have any concerns about our products, you can contact us on

ProductSafety@springernature.com

In case Publisher is established outside the EU, the EU authorized
representative is:

Springer Nature Customer Service Center GmbH
Europaplatz 3
69115 Heidelberg, Germany

www.ingramcontent.com/pod-product-compliance
Ingram Content Group UK Ltd.
Pitfield, Milton Keynes, MK11 3LW, UK
UKHW021256180426
11947UKWH00011B/802